Friends in High Places

Also by Thomas Shepherd

New Thought author and theologian Thomas Shepherd also writes fiction under the pen name Thomas Henry Quell. His latest novel, *The Princess and the Prophet,* is Volume One of a science fiction trilogy currently in the works. T.H. Quell novels are published by iUniverse Press and are available at most retail bookstores and online at various sites including iUniverse.com, Barnes & Noble, and Amazon.com.

Friends in High Places

Tracing the Family Tree of New Thought Christianity

Thomas Shepherd

iUniverse, Inc.
New York Lincoln Shanghai

Friends in High Places
Tracing the Family Tree of New Thought Christianity

Copyright © 2004, 2006 by Thomas W. Shepherd

iUniverse books may be ordered through booksellers or by contacting:

iUniverse
2021 Pine Lake Road, Suite 100
Lincoln, NE 68512
www.iuniverse.com
1-800-Authors (1-800-288-4677)

Third Edition, Revised October 2006.
Originally published as a 12-part *Unity Magazine* series.
First book edition by Unity Books (1985).

Cover Photo
St. Luke the Evangelist stained glass window photo courtesy of P.N. Ralley
(www.stainedglassphotography.com). Used by permission.

ISBN-13: 978-0-595-32534-4 (pbk)
ISBN-13: 978-0-595-66636-2 (cloth)
ISBN-13: 978-0-595-77331-2 (ebk)
ISBN-10: 0-595-32534-3 (pbk)
ISBN-10: 0-595-66636-1 (cloth)
ISBN-10: 0-595-77331-1 (ebk)

Printed in the United States of America

For pastors, toiling in the night to bring new thoughts to the people:

You do not labor alone…

Contents

Foreword by E.J. Niles xi

Introduction: A Short Course in Epistemology xiii

Part I   *Jewish Roots & Christian Branches*

CHAPTER 1   Father of Metaphysical Interpretation 3

CHAPTER 2   Father of Christian Universalism 17

CHAPTER 3   Free Will or Predestination? .29

Part II   *Those Marvelous Medieval Mystics*

CHAPTER 4   Brightness of the Divine Darkness 45

CHAPTER 5   Beyond the Night Sky 58

CHAPTER 6   Spark of the Soul 69

Part III   *Setting the Stage*

CHAPTER 7   The Cheerful Walker 83

CHAPTER 8   First, Second, and Third Force 95

CHAPTER 9   The Bridge Builders 106

Part IV   *Yesterday, Today, and Tomorrow*

CHAPTER 10   Three Women Prophets 121

CHAPTER 11   Shaking the Foundations 131

CHAPTER 12   Faith for the Future 141

Afterword. 153
Selected Bibliography 157
APPENDIX A   Why We're Not A Cult 163
APPENDIX B   Study Guide 177
APPENDIX C   Evolution of the God-Concept 191
About the Author 193
Index 195

Acknowledgements

With many thanks to many "Friends" around the planet. Special thanks to David Anderson, whose keen eye caught an abundance of errors, and to my wife, Carol-Jean, who went over the text meticulously one last time—several *one last times*, actually, while it was being re-written. Working together, they have allowed me to appear a little more scholarly than my natural mental state probably deserves. Thanks also to a genuine scholar, Matthew Fox, who graciously read and offered suggestions about the chapter on Meister Eckhart, but is not to be held responsible for any faux pas in the finished product.

Special thanks also to my many friends, colleagues, students and those angelic souls who responded to my Internet request for assistance from all points along the "Mid-Week Message" mailstring,[1] for helping with an 11th hour, back-from-the-publisher re-check of the proofs. My final-proof angels included: Shirley Bowman, Lauri Boyd, Michael Brooks, Robert Brach, Barry Cravens, William Heller, Margaret Flick, Lou Freeman, Mark Fuss, Michael Jamison, Brad Langdon, Barbara Healing-McInerney, Kelly Isola, Chris Gerbino Kennedy, Nancy Layne, Tom Lee, Joslyn Mason, James A. Pearce, Jr., Kate Joanna Peppler, Robyn Plante, Monya Scherzer, Melinda A. Slater, Edith Washington, Lori A. Woodley, Wendy Zender, and Fred Zydek. If I missed anybody, you are nonetheless beloved by incompetent me and cherished by Omnipotent God.

Finally, special thanks to all the students and faculty of Unity Institute at Unity Village, Missouri, who constantly remind me that, in a truly Christian theology, wisdom and love always trump research and reason.

---

1. To join Rev Tom Shepherd's (free) Mid-Week Message mailstring write: ShepherdMidWkMsg@aol.com with the word ADD in the subject line. Also, visit his website: MetaphysicalTheology.com

FOREWORD

We are living in a time when world conditions are causing people of all religious persuasions to question their faiths, and Christianity is not exempt from this questioning. Voices of concern about the state of Christianity are coming from many quarters. Karen Armstrong in her testimonial to Bishop John Shelby Spong's book, *Why Christianity Must Change or Die*, refers to "the Christian dilemma of our time." In the same book Bishop Spong himself speaks of "religious propaganda, which has its origins in a world that none of us any longer inhabits."[1] And Biblical scholar Burton Mack states, "We are very close to entertaining a public discourse about our nation's Christian heritage that does not rise above the level of demagoguery."[2]

Faced with this kind of concern about the fate of the Christian church, Thomas Shepherd has reminded us that from pre-Christian times to the twentieth century there have been those who carried the torch of optimism, prophets and mystics who reminded us that even unchanging Truth must adapt in response to changing life conditions.

The Christian church has survived through challenges from without and within. From Philo in the first century of the Common Era to Pierre Teilhard de Chardin of the twentieth, there have been those who held to the belief that the Truth is more than what the particular exclusivist or limited teachings of the day proclaimed. They were the sages down through the ages, our *Friends in High Places.*

Tom Shepherd's work is especially valuable to those who consider themselves New Thought Christians in today's post-modern world. Lest we think

---

1. John Shelby Spong, *Why Christianity Must Change or Die* (SF: Harper Collins, 1998), 4.
2. Burton Mack, *Who Wrote the New Testament?* (SF: Harper Collins, 1995), 309.

"New Thought" is new, Shepherd introduces us to men and women who planted seeds of Truth long centuries ago. The harvest is now becoming more visible as New Thought churches and groups are being recognized by such organizations as The Jesus Seminar, and scholars like John Shelby Spong and Matthew Fox. Ideas once considered unique to New Thought are emerging within many Christian denominations, especially the more progressive organizations. These perennial ideas, which could serve as harmonizers among the wildly diverse followers of Jesus, are being considered widely today, some finding their way into the lessons and liturgies of the Christian family of religions.

It is a great time to be a part of the New Thought movement. It is also a great time to reclaim our role in Church history as part of the mystical heritage of western spirituality. Our spiritual ancestors created and passed along profound insights, ideas which would shape New Thought Christianity, and in so doing they have contributed to the fruition of the whole faith in bits and pieces. Those little glimpses of Truth accelerated the evolutionary process and nudged the Christian church along its upwards growth spiral by questioning, not for the first time and certainly not for the last, what it means to be Christian. A good sampling of the men and women who lived that developmental process will spring to life in the pages of this book.

I look forward to other works by Tom Shepherd as he continues his quest to identify, research, and write about our *Friends in High Places*.

E.J. Niles
Unity Institute
September, 2006

Introduction
A Short Course in Epistemology

A lot has happened since Jesus walked the Earth. Wars and rumors of wars, periods of peace and cultural advancement, outpourings of creative genius and terrible repressions against the human spirit. Christianity began in a humble manger and moved up the socio-economic ladder to occupy mighty thrones. Sometimes, Christian theology—which is reflection on the Divine from a Christ-centered perspective—has reached great heights in the drama of life and faith. Other times, theology succumbed to great temptations and sank into pettiness and superstition, a poor performance for a people who see themselves made *imago Dei*, in the image of God.

Yet, even gloomy epochs present opportunities for minor characters to move across the dark stage. The playbill always changes. Meanwhile, countless unknown and lesser-known actors have created their roles in the Divine drama, if only as a walk-on. Sometimes the artist's contribution is a silioquy delivered to an empty house, a monologue of the faith, which the player never knew had been heard by anyone, save God. Notwithstanding the stage scenery of popular belief—which paint the backdrop of early and medieval Christendom as an endless mural of Inquisitions, presided over by an obstreperous cadre of heresy-hunters intent on breaking their innocent victims on the rack—most periods in Church history have actually been a lot more bucolic and ordinary. Most lives were characterized by the quiet, everyday, pastoral work of clergy and the daily drama of individual Christians trying to love and be loved, live and let live, all in the Name of Jesus Christ. However, even the most optimistic church historian will allow that the long history of Christianity has not always been pleasant. Ghosts clamor in the basement, clanking about in great iron chains, always threatening to creep up the back stairs some dark night and catch people unaware. The story continues, and all humanity has been cast in the drama.

Much harm has been done in misbegotten service to the Prince of Peace. Anyone who studies Christian history must begin with a frank admission: humans have not always loved their neighbor as they love themselves. Any study of the Christian faith that does not face the ghosts in the basement will be unable to point to the angels on the balconies. This work intends to look at some of those phantoms and cherubs, with an appropriate emphasis on the good guys, heroes who fought their lonely battles, original thinkers who nudged human consciousness along its painfully slow but unmistakable upward path.

All too often, people reject the whole heritage of Christian theology because of the poltergeists rumbling in the dark cellars of the house of faith. If memories from religious education replay only as dissonant tunes—the banshee cry of an unchecked authoritarianism which demands belief in all manner of nonsense, or the mournful wail of a desultory and moribund traditionalism—a different refrain swells from the pages of this study.

Listen closely, savor another tune from the great symphony of Christian thought. A delicious melody, humming in the background much of the time. Now and again it takes center stage as the whole orchestra seizes the juicy tune and plays it grandly for a season. Then discord rises, and the sweet, persistent melody falls into oblivion once more. Today's generation did not write the music; twenty-first century Christianity has inherited the song of Spirit from its unknown ancestors in the faith. Regrettably, most people have not a clue about the great indebtedness of Christian thought—especially New Thought Christianity—to the unsung heroes and heroines of the past, the great forefathers and foremothers of the mystical heritage. Their music sings in the soul of humanity, yet they remain largely anonymous, lost in the long corridors of history. This work will attempt a first step toward reconciliation with those neglected and forgotten virtuosos of the spiritual orchestra.

Mystical-Metaphysical Christianity

Some New Thought Christians are fond of the word *metaphysical* when describing their studies and spiritual exercises. Another term exists which may better describe the endeavor, a word with a long and distinguished history in Western thought. The word is *mysticism*. Those who practice this way of religion are called *mystics*.

Every faith has produced mystics. Every religious hierarchy has viewed the mystic with mistrust. The mystic usually responded by pronouncing the hierarchy a betrayer of the Faith, and the hierarchy fought back by excommunicating the heretical mystic. Something about mysticism raises the hairs on the back of the neck of religious authority. Perhaps it is because the mystic wants no go between, no priestly figure standing in the holy place, distributing the divine graces. Mystics share an age-old passion to know God personally. To experience God, to feel God's presence, not just read about God in a book, these are the goals of mysticism. Rewards for pursuing the mystical path include higher consciousness and direct inspiration from the Divine. Rather than the sublime God concept of the philosophers, the mystic wants a personal encounter with God. Not the abstract deity of Descartes, Spinoza, and Whitehead, but the intimate, active God who communed with Moses, David, and Jesus. Like the old hymn, mystics hunger for a Lord with whom to walk and talk in the garden of life. Religious organizations, on the other hand, prefer their prophets safely dead, entombed in ancient texts, stained glass and stone, where they may inspire the faithful but deliver no fresh tablets from Sinai which might rock the ark of established doctrine.

Although the lone prophet is a sympathetic figure, in all fairness one needs to acknowledge that religious hierarchies do have a point here. Some sort of check and balance seems necessary against totally individualized beliefs, fanciful ideas which represent theological eccentricity rather than helpful innovation. Yet, if the mystic is correct when affirming Truth comes directly from God, the obvious problem is how to distinguish among contradictory truths. How does an aspiring mystic know when something gleaned in mystical communion is an authentic insight from God and not just a fanciful notion? If recognizing personal divine guidance is sometimes difficult, how much more when the claim is secondhand? How does an open-minded person respond to those who allege they have received special, authoritative revelations from the Divine? Shall religionists take seriously every person who stands and shouts, *"Thus saith the Lord"*?

A Baptist clergyman once said, "Religion is a way for some people to be socially acceptably crazy."[1]Although this sounds a bit harsh, there is an ele-

---

1.   Commented to the author in private conversation with a Baptist colleague during my years as a US Army chaplain, a long time ago in a galaxy far, far away…

Christian writings—they edited out the heresy and filled in the blanks to "correct" errors in the text.

Please note: In their way of thinking these men[6] were usually not coldly rewriting history, blatantly creating false versions of the gospels. They were interpreting and correcting, based on truth which they believed had been handed down to them in Apostolic succession. When presented with an offensive passage in a hand-copied manuscript, scribes often became copy editors. It is not difficult to imagine a devout Ebionite, Gnostic or proto-orthodox copyist mumbling to himself, *"Jesus could NOT have said that!"* So, he softened the remark with alternative, acceptable language, which corrected the error and presented the Truth, i.e., Ebionite, Gnostic or proto-orthodox theology. Because it has been seen as the ultimate authority source in matters of faith and morals, the temptation to re-write the Bible persists today. How often have congregations heard their ministers, priests and rabbis suggest alternative readings, *"Now, what this text is really saying is…"*?

Due to recent manuscript discoveries—like the Coptic library consisting of fifty-two texts discovered in earthen jars at Nag Hammadi in Upper Egypt in 1945—scholars now have better evidence about the intriguing ideas advanced by other groups, the "heresies" who lost their bid to become number one in the early church reality show. Although extraordinary forces shaped the arena in which Christianity grew to maturity—e.g., erosion of the old Roman Republic, the rise of an unchallenged Imperial Rome with its corresponding *Pax Romana* which allowed relatively safe travel on well-built roads and aboard ships in a well-policed Mediterranean Sea; the ascending popularity of cultic mystery religions imported from the Near East to satisfy the ubiquitous hunger for personal immortality in Hellenistic society; and two Jewish wars of rebellion and their consequent violent suppression by Rome—nevertheless, one should not dismiss the idea that a Divine element has also been at work in the evolutionary process. Twenty centuries later Pierre Teilhard de Chardin will propose a direction of flow for the whole process of evolution, from non-living through consciousness to the Omega Point, which he identified with the Christ.

However, not even Teilhard—who was at once Jesuit priest, ground-breaking paleontologist, and unequaled theologian—will argue that everything

---

6. Because they dominated the scribal arts, scholars are fairly sure *men* are to blame.

which happened was the only possible route humanity could have chosen. The fact is, there has never been a single orthodoxy. When Jesus walked among humanity, he was accompanied by at least twelve disciples, each a one-person denomination, endlessly quibbling over doctrine and personal authority. Later his followers, lacking an understanding of the dynamics of religious belief and its healthy tendency toward diversity as theologies evolve, killed each other for want of a unifying vision. After sixteen centuries of this doctrinal squabbling, it is no surprise that a reformer like Luther had to run afoul of a Church hierarchy which demanded *my-way-or-death*.

Today, a significant number of people are inclined to nod when someone repeats the post-modern maxim *Many Paths, One God*. However, Luther had no such vantage point. He attacked beliefs which were different from his own, because he functioned from the premise *one path to one truth*, an idea sometimes stenciled on bumper stickers today with the words *One Way*. Luther had to defend his case in a world which assumed the Catholic Church was the one way to God. The Church had proclaimed itself the direct descendent of Jesus on earth, and this proclamation went unanswered for centuries.

As a theologian Luther realized he could not simply assert this new teaching based on personal insight alone. He called upon a large number of witnesses to testify on behalf of the case he was trying to make, great thinkers and teachers who saw that faith rather than works in the outer world was the key to salvation. The Church countered with centuries of tradition, Canon Law and a vast army of historic figures who stood with the Pope. Luther called as his chief witness the Judeo-Christian Bible, and he demanded the right to interpret Scripture with a free mind. Making such a demand for himself, he could hardly deny the same privileges to others. Luther opened the door to individual freedom, and the Protestant church fled with him.

Although the issues of Luther's day no longer incite riots as they did in sixteenth century Europe, the same questions dog the heels of creative theologians today. The Catholic Church banned the writings of Teilhard during his lifetime and more recently silenced the Liberation Theology movement and fired free-thinking theologians like Matthew Fox. Lest the Catholic hierarchy take all the credit for mismanagement of creative thinking, conservative Protestants have added their voices to the anti-progressive backlash by decrying Episcopal Bishop John Shelby Spong and other members of the *Jesus Seminar* as heretics, while demanding public schools teach children a pre-scientific worldview which is contrary to the discoveries of physical science, world history and cultural anthropology. To turn inside-out St. Anthony's comment about abandoning society for safety in the Church, small wonder if thinking men and women of today abandon the Church like it was a shipwreck from which survivors must swim for their lives.

The Word for Today is *"Epistemology…"*

In both philosophy and theology, the discipline which asks, *"How do we know what's true?"* is called *epistemology*. Whether drafting a brief monograph or launching a *magnum opus*, epistemology is the first question all philosophers and theologians must address, albeit unconsciously, before sitting down to write.

In the centuries before the current era, religious thinkers liked to codify their convictions by composing creeds and confessions. The theory was that if they could boil down all the theological verbiage into a clear essence, usually by writing an official creed or less formal statement of faith, the resulting document would both clarify the beliefs and provide educational guidance for the community of faith. Sometimes this goal seems to have been achieved with a minimum of discomfort to non-conformists, even with the possibility of adjustment as consciousness changes, as with the United Church of Christ's *Statement of Faith*. "The UCC receives historic statements of faith as 'testimonies, not tests…'" proclaims the denominational website.[7] To its credit, the UCC has tried diligently to live with the discomfort of diversity and resisted the temptation to require uniformity of belief.

However, too often churches have adopted official statements then insisted that everyone abide by the words of the creed as a way of insuring everyone would get to heaven. In the not-too-far-distant past, churchmen felt justified in torturing people to force agreement with official written doctrine. It all made sense when starting from the premise of divine punishment awaiting sinful humanity in the fires of hell. If immortal souls were at stake, what rational person would not trade a few hours of agony for the guarantee of eternal bliss? The poverty of this line of thought is obvious from the vantage point of this post-modern age. Humanity has a miserable track record at attaining perfect statements of faith but a long history of inflicting torture upon men and women anyway.

---

7. UCC *Statement of Faith* (1959) was revised for more inclusive language by Robert Moss, then revised again as a Doxology in 1983.

Creeds and confessions fail to take into account the evolutionary nature of human consciousness. Succeeding generations change and grow while creeds remain static. As Harry Emerson Fosdick said early in the twentieth century:

> The fact that astronomies change while the stars abide is a true analogy of every realm of human life and thought, religion not least of all. No existent theology can be a final formulation of spiritual Truth.[8]

Today, instead of perfect statements that will be true forever, the departure point for most theologies is an epistemology based on guiding principles that interact with each other dialectically. Not a voice from Mount Olympus, but a workshop. Not one way alone to interpret the ancient faith, but a series of important factors to consider involving theology today or at any time in the future.

Posting a Model for Post-Modern Mystics

Another large protestant body, the United Methodist Church, has suggested a dialectical system based on four poles of reference. Instead of standing on any one authority source, this dynamic approach to epistemology recognizes at least four reference points for doing theology. This model, known popularly as the Methodist Quadrilateral, brings ideas into dialogue within four great sources of theological reflection: *Scripture, tradition, experience,* and *reason.*

These reference points interact so efficiently that no single source, such as the Bible, is allowed to overwhelm the others. In fact, a person is free to let these four be in conflict with each other, as they often are in reality, without feeling disloyal to the Christian faith. Are there ideas in the Bible which people find repulsive to reason and life experience? Are events happening in the world today against which the biblical witness cries out? Does the power of reason contradict a traditional idea, or does a church tradition provide such a cozy comfort zone that some people want to give themselves permission to enjoy it, perhaps because this particular institutional habit offers solace and reminds people of God's gracious love?

---

8.   Harry Emerson Fosdick, http://www.brainyquote.com/quotes/authors/h/harry_emerson_fosdick.html

Although Quadrilateral allows a mix-and-match theology, it is not a license to be irresponsible, because a balanced theology will employ all four in dialogue with each other. Martin Luther emphasized the Bible so much that the great cry of the Reformation became, *"Sola Scriptura!"* (Only the Scripture). On closer examination, one can see that Luther used reason, experience, and the ideas of other theologians (tradition) when constructing his theological framework.

Sooner or later, every religious organization and every believer must face the question of epistemology: *"How do we know what's true?"* The problem is complicated in Western thought after Luther, whose willingness to think independently and to break with tradition implicitly gave everyone else the right to do likewise; most Reformers who followed Luther held the deep conviction that every person can *"go to headquarters"* as Charles Fillmore did. He found the religious scene of late nineteenth century Christianity as confusing as Martin Luther had encountered early in the sixteenth. Like Luther, Fillmore decided people need no institutions to tell them what God wants them to know. Scripture can be read and interpreted through divine inspiration; the Kingdom of God can be discovered within individual consciousness. Fillmore and Luther both withdrew into private study and meditation where they received illumination by which they lived the rest of their lives and changed the lives of many other people.

Both pioneers opened doors to let fresh air and sunlight into a stagnant house of faith. Both faced the charge of heresy and of inventing a new religion, which they both hotly denied. Fillmore's declaration could have flowed from Luther's pen:

> The Truth we teach is not new, neither do we claim special discovery of new religious principles. Our purpose is to help and teach mankind to use and prove the eternal Truth taught by the Master.[9]

When playing the religion game, Metaphysical Christianity has a great batting average with three of the four elements of the four-point model suggested. New Thought people have made great strides toward a post-modern understanding of *Scripture,* thanks to great Bible teachers—like E.J. Niles of

---

9.   Charles Fillmore, *Unity Magazine,* August 1986. This quote is one of Mr. Fillmore's best-known remarks and appears frequently in Unity publications.

Unity Institute and Dr. Mary Tumpkin of the UFBL—and are comfortable pairing the historical-critical context with "metaphysical" interpretations gleaned from studying the cryptic symbolism of Hebrew and Greek words. New Thought Christians never shirk from learning from *experience*, and readily engage the power of *reason* in both intuitive/right-brain and intellectual/left-brain thinking—home run every time.

But bring the average New Thought person up to bat against that old devil *tradition* and it's usually *strike three called*. Metaphysical Christians are often emigrants from other spiritual lands. Divine Science, Religious Science, Unity, the UFBL and other New Thought denominations tend to be refugee churches, consequently people from these groups sometimes have a tendency to stigmatize the traditional Church like fleeing Israelites looking backward over their shoulders at captivity in Egypt-land. So, the word *tradition* understandably leaves a bad taste in many people's mouths. That, of course, is a complete misunderstanding of what the traditional Church really is. There is no need to cast the whole Christian heritage overboard because of inherited theological problems.

Déjà vu

Metaphysical interpretation of the Scriptures, which finds root meanings of biblical words then searches for deeper insights through allegory? That method was created by Philo Judaeus in the first century C.E. All people will be transformed spiritually—there is no hell, and all people are basically good? Hardly a new idea. Origen said that in the second century C.E.. And to be sure people got the message, Pelagius said it again in the fifth. God and humanity are one? Christ consciousness the goal? Old stuff, my friends, available in the writings of medieval churchmen like John Scotus Erigena and Meister Eckhart.

In fact, one would be hard pressed to name a single spiritual teaching held by Metaphysical Christianity today not proclaimed by theologians of an earlier age. After a proper introduction to the mystical side of Church history, readers of New Thought literature today should be reeling under a huge dose of déjà vu. It will sound like a song heard before...many times.

Those who seek a mystical path to God today stand as heirs to a long heritage of spiritual theology as ancient and traditional as any other element in the many schools of Christian thought. Too long have mystical Christians allowed the hyper-orthodox and fundamentalist fringe to crowd them off the field of

Church history. Too readily have they abandoned their rightful place as a legitimate school of thought in the diverse household of Christianity. Mysticism is as old as the Bible, and its insights are as "traditional" as those of less contemplative branches of the faith. It is time mystical Christianity reclaimed that heritage.

But how to find that mystical heritage? If there is a long history of teachers and thinkers who have inclined toward a theology of God's goodness, wouldn't it be nice to know who they were? Wouldn't it be a joy to learn that Mystical-Metaphysical Christians are just as orthodox as the highly liturgical neighbors down the street? Furthermore, wouldn't it be delightful to learn that some of the teachings which New Thought Christianity has been proclaiming for over a century are *just now* coming up on the agenda for serious discussion in modern theology?

Wouldn't New Thought people be amazed to discover the time for Mystical-Metaphysical Christianity has not yet fully arrived, because the little melody humming in the wings is gaining strength once more, and widely divergent people today may be singing the opening bars to a whole symphony of ideas which will harmonize the Christian faith with other world religions in the twenty-first century and beyond?

If this scenario sounds appealing, you are cordially invited to read on and be amazed, surprised, and delighted. Believe it or not, you are about to meet a whole pack of strangers who will sound very familiar to you. They are your long-lost relatives in the ancient faith. They are the angels on the balconies of Christendom. They are your *Friends in High Places.*

I

Jewish Roots & Christian Branches

1

Father of Metaphysical Interpretation

Philo Judaeus
(First Century, C.E.)

He paused, pondering the problem, as scribes waited with pen in hand for the rabbi to resume dictation. Beneath the window of his study, merchants hawked trade goods from the farthest corners of the Roman Empire. Spicy smells of noonday cooking—leeks frying in olive oil, lamb roasting over a spit, freshly baked bread—rose from the twisted streets and alleys of the great city around him. Built three hundred years earlier by Alexander the Great, first century Alexandria stood second only to Rome as a commercial and population center. As an intellectual center, it stood second to none.

The library at Alexandria is best known for its archives; it housed the finest collection of ancient manuscripts the world has ever known, but this special place was more than a laboratory and book repository. It was a lyceum, a forum for learning and discourse. The library offered religious shrines, temples, and an assortment of schools, and would be remembered as the first place on Earth to encourage organized research into the biological and physical sciences. Theological ideas from across the wide, pluralistic Greco-Roman world were celebrated and debated here. Hellenism, that elegant, cosmopolitan mixture of classical Greek thought and Roman practicality, found its highest expression at Alexandria, where oriental mystery cults rubbed shoulders with sophisticated schools of Greek philosophy in an atmosphere of free exchange and exciting new ideas.

Yet, this ancient metropolis provided fertile ground for more than just a host of pagan cults and philosophies; Judaism thrived here, too. Classical writers claimed the Jewish population numbered one million in Egypt, most of them living in Alexandria. Although scholars have questioned this astronomical figure, they generally agree that an enormous number of Jews dwelled in Egypt-land at Alexandria.[1] In the days of Jesus, Jews represented one-tenth of the population of the Roman Empire, perhaps as many as eight million. Most of them lived away from the Holy Land in places like Alexandria, Babylon, even Rome.

What has Athens to do with Jerusalem?

It was one of the Children of Israel who paused that day to reflect on the relationship between his two worlds. His name is Philo, but he will be known as *Philo Judaeus* or Philo of Alexandria. Son of a wealthy Jewish family, weaned on the Torah and nurtured by Greek classics, he learned to love both; yet to most people the two worldviews seemed irreconcilable. What connection could there be between the world of Homer, Plato, and Aristotle and that of Abraham, Jacob, and Moses? Is any link possible? Some thought not. Two centuries later the fiery church father Tertullian will cry:

> *What has Athens to do with Jerusalem? What has the Academy to do with the Church?...Away with all attempts to produce a Stoic, Platonic, and dialectic Christianity!*[2]

Voices in Judaism also raised the cry against any conspiracy to Hellenize the faith of Israel. Yet, Philo believed two countervailing worldviews, which are by themselves true, must somehow speak with the same voice. He found divine insights in classical literature and great philosophical truth on every page of the Bible. His problem was how to find a common denominator for Greek and Hebrew thought, a thread he could use to sew together these two vastly different views. Philo believed truth is one. Based on study and personal experience, Philo believed the profound insights of Greek thought were true,

---

1. Samuel Sandmel, *Philo of Alexandria* (New York: Oxford University Press, 1979), 6-7.
2. Paul Johnson, *A History of Christianity* (New York: Atheneum, 1980), 48.

but he also believed in Judaism and its one God. To reject one in favor of the other was an impossible choice for Philo. Philosophy was too logical, too self-evident, to be false, and for a pious Jew to abandon the transcendent God of Israel was equally unthinkable.

Quite reasonably he deduced that, since truth is one, the unspeakably holy *YHWH*—the *I AM* revealed by Hebrew Scripture—must also be the *Logos* or Divine Mind of Greek philosophy. Somewhere there had to be a key concept which unlocked the corridor between these two different worlds. But what key? How could a faithful son of Israel find a bridge between the thought world of Moses and, in Philo's own words, the teachings of "most holy Plato"?[3]

Philo's keen intellect ranged over the vast field of classical studies learned since his boyhood in Alexandria. There, in the works of the great Stoic masters, was the answer. With this key Philo opened the door to modern metaphysical interpretation of the Bible. He single-handedly crafted the basic method which "metaphysical" interpreters have employed ever since. And he did it in the first century.

Zeno's Painted Portico

The key concept was, of course, literary interpretation by use of *allegory*. An allegory is an imaginative explanation of deeper concepts beneath the literal meanings by use of symbolism. Allegory is a creative, interactive process, not unlike viewing art or listening to music, in which patrons of the art participate with the artist by responding from the depth of their consciousness to experience the artist's work with fresh eyes, ears, and hearts. Philo probably learned the method from the Stoics, a school of philosophy popular in his day. Stoicism was based on the teachings of Zeno, issued from his famous painted portico *(stoa* in Greek) at Athens.[4]

Zeno lived in the Third and Fourth Centuries B.C.E., and his teachings were still immensely popular in Philo's first century, C.E. Zeno had taught harmony with all things, a sort of early divine order, and affirmation of the good in the face of apparent evil. The noble Stoic tried to rise above the petty problems of life. English-speaking people today still speak of someone who

---

3.   David Winston, *Philo of Alexandria* (New York: Paulist Press, 1981), 2.
4.   Dagobert D. Runes, (ed.), *Treasury of World Philosophy* (Patterson, NJ: Littlefield, Adams & Co., 1959), 1256.

endures great trials with silent courage as being *stoical*. They also developed a keen sense of moral uprightness. In their sobriety and overbearing sense of ethical rectitude, Stoics were the forerunners of the English Puritans. Little has been preserved from Zeno's writings, but a surviving fragment suggests Stoic harmony:

> To live in accordance with nature is to live in accordance with virtue.
> In doing so, the wise man secures a happy and peaceful course to his own life.[5]

As children of classical Greek culture, the puritanical Stoics had a serious problem with the literature of their religious heritage. Gods and goddesses of Greek and Roman mythology often behaved scandalously. One deity steals another's wife, begetting illegitimate children by her. Another divine player wades into the thick of combat and kills humans for the sheer joy of killing; still others lie, cheat, and steal to obtain their selfish aims. The noble Stoics rebelled against this sub-human behavior on the part of their divinities. However, rather than cast aside the great literature of Greek civilization, cultural treasures like Homer's *Iliad* and *Odyssey*, the Stoics developed a method of interpreting religious literature allegorically.

Such risqué' episodes were not historical events, the Stoics assured one another. They were meant to be taken symbolically, representative of deeper, hidden truths. So, when the *god of war* seizes the *goddess of beauty*, one could see in this an allegory about the loss of innocent youth as the maturing soul (goddess of beauty) comes in contact with the struggles of life (god of war). Allegory saved the day for the Stoics, or at least saved them from the necessity of turning all those statues of the gods and goddesses into birdbaths and garden decorations.

Literalism Not an Option

Philo faced a similar dilemma. He had great difficulty with a literal reading of many parts of the Jewish Scriptures. He was too much a philosopher to consider the option of literalism, so he decided to look deeper by use of allegory. It is a method still employed today.

---

5.   Ibid., 1257.

Freed by allegory, Philo found common ground for Hellenistic thought on the holy ground of the Torah. In Philo's hands, Moses became the greatest of philosophers, the originator of truths taught by later Greek thinkers such as Plato. This reading back into the works of venerable old masters the ideas current in one's own time was a practice common to the Platonic school, especially to Middle Platonism of Philo's day. With typically Hellenistic freedom of thought, pagan commentators were already doing this in first century Alexandria. To defend their own Middle Platonist doctrines, philosophers reinterpreted Plato and extracted from his words the support they needed.

Philo noted with interest what his pagan contemporaries were doing, deciding that reinterpretation of ancient words was a valid academic enterprise. Philo scholar David Winston says this was just what the philosopher ordered:

> Armed with Greek allegorical exegesis (interpretation), which seeks out hidden meanings that lie beneath the surface of any particular text, and given the Middle Platonist...penchant to read back new doctrines into the works of a venerable figure of the past, Philo was fully prepared to do battle for his ancestral tradition.[6]

Best of Two Worlds

And what a battle he fought. Philo's irrepressible energy and vast knowledge produced an endless stream of volumes which blended what he considered the best in Hellenism with the eternal verities of the Hebrew faith. His work gained him such prominence in the Jewish world that he lead the delegation to plead the cause of Jews everywhere, taking his argument to the very courtyard of Caesar. Philo's life story is as exciting as his pioneering work in metaphysical writing, so this study shall investigate each of them.

Philo wrote so much that a mere sounding will have to suffice. The backbone of his work is biblical commentary, which Philo confined to the Torah, or Pentateuch, the first five books of the Hebrew Bible. He wrote much more than this, composing letters, treatises, and whole volumes in defense of Judaism that went beyond biblical commentary. Most of these were sent as one way communications or have not been preserved because their content did not interest the copyists of later ages. However, what remains of Philo's writings is

---

6. Winston, 6.

more than enough to fill several volumes. It is to biblical commentary Philo returns again and again. He must have considered this his *magnum opus*—the great lifework of an energetic and devout religionist.

Sandmel explains how he worked: "Philo utilizes the supposed meaning of the Hebrew names so as to assign an allegorical entity, and this allegorical entity deals with the names as related to the senses, or the passions, or the mind, or the soul, or to proper logic."[7] Philo took the root meanings of the words in a biblical passage and played with them until he found connections between the words of Scripture and the teachings of Plato. Sandmel believes the rabbi did this in all innocence.

> Philo would never have admitted to reading Plato into Scripture, he would have insisted that the Platonism and Stoicism came out of Scripture. He and his Christian successors assert that Philo was right because Plato derived his views from Moses, who was earlier and greater than Plato.[8]

No matter how innocently he proceeded, it is fairly obvious to contemporary readers that Philo radically Platonized the Jewish Scripture, finding Platonic imagery under every stone, turning the legends of Israel into a Judean Odyssey. Yet, in defense of his methodology, one could contend that all literary interpretation is a creative interaction between the words of a long-dead author and the understandings of modern readers. Because Philo assumed Truth is one, he probably would have agreed it is legitimate to "hear" in the words of Scripture messages the author never intended to convey. Art is interactive. Because each human being is unique, every work of chisel, paint or pen will speak with a different voice to every person who contemplates it.

Perhaps one should not be too critical of him for "Philoizing" Plato. Creative interaction with the text can yield good results, even if the author did not have this in mind. As the preface to the *Metaphysical Bible Dictionary* says:

> Our real aim is to assist in leading the student into the inner or spiritual interpretation of the Bible, that he may apply it in the very best and most practical way in his own life.... We are always pleased

---

7.   Sandmel, 28.
8.   *Ibid.*

when anyone learns to go within and get his inspiration direct from his own indwelling Lord or Spirit of Truth.[9]

Dangers & Delights of Metaphysical Interpretation

When Exodus 3:1 says Moses came to the mountain, reflective thinkers might discover a deeper meaning than the wearisome figure of a tired old holy man climbing a hill. It could mean, among other things, that the evolutionary process (Moses)[10] in human consciousness was raised to a higher level, an "exalted state of mind where the divine plan may be perceived and unfolded,"[11] as suggested by Charles Fillmore. The possibilities for allegorical interpretation are virtually unlimited, yet offer special challenges.

Although the goal of spiritual study is certainly to inspire individuals to discover the Power within themselves and find new insights about their relationship to God, not every written work takes the hard-learned lessons of history seriously. Too many books, written for today's popular market, begin with the spurious, neo-Gnostic premise of disclosing secret knowledge. *"Now, Dear Reader, I will reveal to you the secret, hidden key which unlocks the true meaning of the ancient text, which Church leaders have obscured to suppress Truth and maintain their power for all these centuries..."* This approach can be found on the shelves of most bookstores, and it is utter nonsense.

Books written from this vacuous, New-Agey hermeneutic do a disservice to those who are attempting to continue the tradition of metaphysical interpretation. There is no *"secret, hidden key"* which unlocks the *"true"* meaning of the ancient text. There are only present-day reflections on the language, culture, history and symbolism of the time in which the ancient documents were composed, edited, re-edited, and hand-copied multitudinous times. Ancient authors were writing for their market, not for today's. Although there are portions of Scripture which scream to be taken symbolically—the whole book of Revelation, for example—it is more likely that, when the unknown author of Exodus 3:1 penned those words about Moses climbing the mountain, he meant *Moses climbed the mountain.*

---

9. Charles Fillmore, *Metaphysical Bible Dictionary* (Kansas City, MO: Unity Books, 1942), 8.
10. Fillmore, *MDB*, 461.
11. Fillmore, *The Revealing Word* (Unity Village, MO: Unity Books, 1979), 136.

Consequently, to understand what the biblical authors were saying to their target audience, the biblical reader today must understand the issues and goals of the times in which the documents were produced. That is why theological seminaries, including Unity Institute, teach historical backgrounds of the Bible as an integral part of the overall curriculum for biblical studies.

Certainly, the Bible can be interpreted without first understanding its historical context, but often the result is a free-floating, hyper-spiritualized and speculative interpretation which may have little to do with what the text is actually saying. While there is nothing wrong with just reading the words without regard for context, the depth of understanding which can be achieved when apprehending the probable intent of the ancient author(s) will pay spiritual dividends to those who take the time to invest in careful study and critical reflection.

The amazing power of symbolism is that, even in the twenty-first century, the assortment of mental utensils provided by ancient writers allow people to grasp the spiritual issues of the present day. Metaphysical (allegorical) interpretation can help, but only if grounded in history and only if people today frankly admit they are usually not discovering hidden secrets but co-creating something new.

The danger of allegory is as noteworthy as its delights. Religious symbolism presents a value-neutral tool which can serve diverse causes, like peace or violence, as anyone who has studied world history will attest. Any symbol can be abused, its power brought to bear for causes which sensible people recognize as evil goals. The cross—which has been and continues to be a deeply mystical symbol for the Presence and Power of God regardless of circumstances to the contrary—has nevertheless been invoked by less appealing causes, like the Crusades, Nazi's, and the KKK. Theologian Matthew Fox makes an important point when he says the place where sunlight shines brightest will often cast the darkest shadow.[12]

When applying the art of symbolic interpretation to sacred literature, the dangers are magnified, because the Scriptures have such power to command the attention of so many people. The temptation persists to re-interpret passages to make the text support this or that opinion, for the good or ill. For this reason, one could argue that every interpreter must be clear about the theological presuppositions from which he or she operates. It is no accident that a

---

12. Comments by Matthew Fox at Unity Institute, Summer 2006.

Russian Orthodox clergyman and a Mormon missionary reading the same biblical passage about the priesthood will come away with vastly different understandings of its symbolic undertone.

This tendency to import meaning to the text is an almost unshakable natural consequence of owning and operating a human brain. People seldom go to their holy scriptures to *get* religion; more often readers go to the Torah, New Testament, or Koran with their religious worldviews fully deployed in search of corroborating information. The word for this misuse of Holy Writ is *proof-texting*, and almost everybody is guilty of it to some degree, especially those who deny it most vehemently. The place to begin any work of symbolic interpretation therefore is with a frank admission of one's theological presuppositions.

Lectio Divina

Of course, as indicated above, people can also open sacred scripture to read purely for inspiration without any sort of historical exegesis; that kind of devotional reading is sometimes called *Lectio Divina*. The *Lectio* is an ancient and important practice because, through reading and reflecting on words considered sacred, readers engage in spiritual opening to whatever insights God may have for them. This is done without readers pretending they possess some kind of code key to decipher the true meaning of the text. *Lectio* is an avenue for communion with God, a reflective, non-interpretative reading that encourages prayer and meditation, which Philo also thought was an important goal of sacred studies. *Lectio Divina* might also include meditation on symbols in the text, not for the purpose of discovering some concealed significance but simply to hear God's voice anew through the imagery of scripture. In the best of all worlds, however, an understanding of the historical context will enrich even the most casual reading of scripture.

The 'Grand Allegory'

To his credit, Philo attempted to do it all—provide spiritual insights, marry them with the science and philosophy of his day, and encourage individuals to pray and meditate on sacred truths. And he did his vast work in no haphazard way. His deftness at handling even the most obtrusive scriptural passages is uncanny, yet he has a method to his metaphysics. The commentary moves through allegory after allegory—an endless stream of symbolism—toward what Sandmel calls the *Grand Allegory*.

Everything in Philo moves majestically toward his goal for all humanity, which is mystical communion with God. Philo is a true mystic, not just an abstract speculator. Mysticism is an ancient form of religiosity found in many religious traditions, Western and otherwise. The mystic recognizes no intermediary between himself and God. For him, access to God is always direct and personal. Sometimes mystical experience takes the form of meditation or prayer, but it can also include dance, song, ecstatic utterance, or vision-questing.

Mysticism can be the cool reflection of a Trappist monk in his hermitage or the passionate cries and holy dance of Hasidic Jews in the streets of Jerusalem. The key ingredient in mysticism is involvement by the worshiper directly with God. The mystic is seized by God and, conversely, God is seized by the mystic. Together God and the human dance, commune, interact. The aim of mysticism is union with God.

This is the key to understanding Philo, for mystical union with God underlies virtually every sentence, every bit of his interpretive dream weaving. Philo deeply believed that Plato and Moses were both teaching ways for humanity to commune with the one true God. He used allegory for mystical and theological purposes, attempting to provide ways for the worshiper to tear down the walls separating man and God. For him, the events of Scripture are intimate encounters, happening in everyone's spiritual life, like parables of soul growth. Nineteen centuries later Charles Fillmore will write: "The fact is that the entire theme of the Bible is man and his various states of mind, represented as persons, tents, tabernacles, temples."[13]

Today's readers who delve into Philo's writings may often find themselves forgetting they were written almost two thousand years ago by a Greek-speaking Jew. Philo frequently uses terms which overlap with language common to New Thought literature. His allegory of the patriarchs Enoch and Noah uses exactly the same root meanings as can be found in the *Metaphysical Bible Dictionary*.

Enoch represents *repentance*, and Noah symbolizes *tranquility* in both Philo and Fillmore. Philo speaks of a "higher mystery" and a "lower mystery," which

---

13. Charles Fillmore, *Atom-Smashing Power of Mind* (Unity Village, MO: Unity Books, 1949), 80.

New Thought authors call levels of consciousness. He suggests that the soul, upon death, may be reabsorbed into universal consciousness or, in a quaint note reflecting both his openness and his limited astronomical knowledge, he wonders if it might enter a star.[14]

The Philo Road Show: Playing Caesar's Palace

Philo's life was not just the quiet pursuits of a lonely scholar. He was a powerful force in Alexandrian society due to his family's prosperity and his status as a great teacher. Philo's nephew, Alexander, became a Roman general. In Hellenistic society, Jews often rose to high rank and position.

Fortunately Philo did not live to *see* the Jews of Palestine rebel against Rome in C.E. 70. The horror of knowing that the Temple had been destroyed by Roman soldiers would have brought double pain to Philo, since his nephew, General Alexander, commanded the Roman forces which took the city.

Philo became a spokesperson for more than just Alexandrian Judaism; the controversy about the place of Jews in the Empire overtook him. After severe rioting took place during which Jews were killed at Alexandria, Philo led a delegation to Rome to set their position before Caesar and asked for justice and protection under Roman law. It was Philo's misfortune that these incidents took place during the reign of Emperor Gaius Julius Caesar Augustus Germanicus, known to popular history as Caligula. Today, Caligula is best remembered as the Emperor who tried to make his horse a member of the Senate, who sold the wives and daughters of the Senators into public prostitution, and who proclaimed himself a living god. Other Caesars allowed themselves to be worshipped as symbols of the Roman State; some historians believe Caligula actually thought he *was* an Olympian deity. It was before this megalomaniac that genteel, scholarly Philo presented his case.

Philo tells what happened during the audience with Caligula. First the Jew-hating Isidorus spoke, ranting about how dangerous and disloyal Philo's people were. Philo and his delegation began to speak in defense of Judaism, but the Emperor seemed more interested in the building project going on around them than the fate of one-tenth of his subjects. Several times during the heat of discussions Caligula jumped up and ran off to bark orders in the room next door about the shape of new windows or some other renovation.

---

14. Sandmel, 84, 88, 100.

Although the debate was supposed to concern only the Jews of Alexandria, Philo quickly realized that, in the attention-deficient mind of the Emperor, "…the fate of all the Jews everywhere should rest on us five envoys."[15]

Jewish Exemption

In Philo's judgment, the very existence of his people might be at stake. Though a tense encounter, Caligula apparently did not have the presence of mind to follow the debate. At one point in the proceedings, while discussing citizenship of Jews in the Empire, Caligula interrupted them and, in Philo's words, "He put to us this grave and momentous question, 'Why do you refuse to eat pork?'"[16]

Philo feared the Jewish cause was in deep trouble. Fortunately, the quicksilver mind of the Emperor refused to dally with such trivialities as the fate of the Jewish population when important matters like the shape of windows had to be decided.

Caligula summarily dismissed the case, decreeing that Jews "…seem to be people unfortunate rather than wicked."[17]

This ended the audience.

When Caligula was soon murdered by his own people, Philo probably saw it as divine retribution. However, Philo's legation to Caesar did have a positive effect. Jews were eventually afforded full protection under Roman law as long as they did not rebel. They were freed from, the requirement to worship the Emperor's image—which was a large concession—and from the order to hang graven images of Caesar in Jewish public places such as the temple and their synagogues. Jews were also free from compulsory military service, except that a Roman soldier marching by a Jew could lawfully require him to carry the Roman's pack one mile.

This is, of course, the background for the teaching of Jesus in Matthew 5:41: "And if any one forces you to go one mile, go with him two miles."[18]

---

15. *Ibid.,* 46.
16. *Ibid.*
17. *Ibid.*
18. *Revised Standard Version.*

Philo's Influence on Christian Thought

Philo's legacy in theological circles was profound as well. He opened the doors to metaphysical interpretation of the Bible even before the New Testament was written. He pioneered method of interpretation which allows the creative spirit to flow through those doors even today.

Every generation has faced the challenge to reinterpret the Bible and remake the ancient faith in symbolic understandings which would speak to each new age. New insights stream forth as humanity continues its upward quest for truth and creative expression. Philo offered the basic outline for what would become metaphysical Bible interpretation when he wedded Stoic allegory to Platonic concepts and applied them to the Bible many years ago.

He lived in the ancient world as a devout Jew and a subscriber to Hellenism's classical philosophies. He believed some things which seem quaint and peculiar to people today. Yet, the basic thread running through the works of Philo Judaeus is mystical/metaphysical. Philo's methodology never caught on in orthodox Judaism, which continued busily building a wall to shut out foreign influences and preserve its ancient heritage. In all fairness to rabbinic Judaism, one must admit that those practices of endogamy, fastidious dietary rules and codes of conduct advocated by the Pharisees did allow Judaism to survive in an increasingly hostile non-Jewish world.

Philo died before the destructive Roman responses to the Jewish Wars of 70 and 132 C.E., so he was out of step with the hard realities of Jewish survival. Philo has never been popular among rabbinic scholars and commentators. In his lifetime occupation as a neo-Platonist biblical interpreter, he tried to swim upstream against the main current of thought in his community of faith, and remains out of the Jewish mainstream today.

But Philo lived on the cusp of another era. There was a new kid on the block among world faiths, a movement sizzling with vitality and eager to share its insights with all humanity, Jew and Gentile alike. It will be this vibrant, innovative, sometimes arrogant, new faith springing from Jewish roots which will replant Philo's allegories in the garden of popular religious faith. In fact, Christian scholarship has taken such a keen interest in this ancient Jewish author that in the year 2000 conservative Christian publisher Wm. B. Eerdmans issued a 371-page, hard-bound concordance, *The Philo Index: A Complete Word Index to the Writings of Philo of Alexandria.*[19]

Some Christians have discovered in Philo the last great prophet before the coming of Jesus Christ, despite the fact that he outlived Jesus and died in the mid-first century, probably hearing little or nothing about the obscure Messiah from Nazareth. Even so, Philo's biblical interpretations opened doors that Christian scholars would rush through in the generations to come.

The next study voyages beyond Hellenistic Judaism to re-discover a man who has been called the greatest intellectual in church history. It will be Origen, the brilliant and controversial North African Christian, who nurtures Philo's arguments beyond their Jewish genesis through to a maturing concept of Christian universalism.

---

19. Peder Borgen, Kare Fuglseth & Roald Skasten, *The Philo Index: A Complete Word Index to the Writings of Philo of Alexandria* (Grand Rapids, MI: Wm. B. Eerdman's Publishing Company, 2000).

2

Father of Christian Universalism

Origen of Alexandria
(Second Century C.E.)

Philo Judaeus lived until about C.E.50, just as Paul was beginning his mission to the Gentiles, before any New Testament book was written. To his dying day Philo remained a staunch advocate of Hellenized Judaism, a true believer in the oneness of Plato's Divine Mind with Yahweh, the God of Israel. Yet the mystical Judaism Philo taught with such passion failed to persuade the majority of the Jews in the late ancient world. Jewish mysticism would continue as a minority viewpoint within rabbinic Judaism until the flowering of medieval Jewish thought produced one of the finest mystical documents the world has ever known, the *Kabala*.

With the destruction of the Temple in C.E. 70 by forces commanded by Philo's nephew, the apostate Alexander, Judaism became introverted, pessimistic about the world, and more concerned with miniscule rulings on every facet of daily life than mystics such as Philo would have wanted. Rabbinic Judaism provided an interpretive mosaic which gave color and depth to everyday life for ordinary Jews living in an increasingly hostile world. During the closing days of the first century and the beginning of the Second, that world was to become almost unbearable for the Children of Israel.

Rome drove the Jews from its city precincts in C.E. 90, but the final blow to Jewish optimism came in C.E. 132, during the Second Jewish War. The revolt broke out in Jerusalem, led by Simon bar Kocheba, who was crowned as the Messiah by the illustrious Rabbi Akiba after the rebellion's initial success. The intoxication brought about by freedom from Roman rule led Jerusalem to

17

proclaim the state of Israel reestablished, even to strike a coin commemorating *Simon, Prince of Israel.* Dancing in the streets ended abruptly as Rome responded with overwhelming might and devastating cruelty. Jerusalem fell once more.

Roman rule was usually tolerant in regard to religious practices and bitterly cruel in the face of insurrection or armed uprising. Having endured rebellion after rebellion from that quarter of their Empire, Roman patience was totally exhausted in the Second Jewish War of C.E. 132. The entire population of Jerusalem was crucified in unspeakably brutal reprisal. Roman executioners ran out of wood for crucifixions and had difficulty finding enough level ground to erect all the crosses they had built. The Romans not only devastated Jewish Jerusalem, they built a pagan temple at the site of Solomon's splendid House of the Lord on Mount Zion, and eternally banned any Jew from coming near Jerusalem proper.[1]

One wonders if the words of Jesus might have echoed in the minds of the people involved in this great catastrophe, almost like words of personal advice, given just a century before within the gates of ruined Jerusalem:

> But I say to you, Do not resist an evildoer. But if anyone strikes you on the right cheek, turn the other also…Love your enemies and pray for those who persecute you.[2]

"You are all one in Christ Jesus…"

As Judaism was retreating behind its cultural walls, the Christian community was reaching out to Hellenistic society with almost reckless abandon. No sector of life was too high or too low for evangelists like Paul and his disciples; the second century church had followed in his footsteps. Women, slaves, freedmen—all persons of traditionally lower status in the male-dominated Roman society—became full members of the Christian church, equal to landed gentry or military commanders or even high officials of the government.

---

1. Jonas C. Greenfield, "The History of Israel, Part I," *The Interpreter's One Volume Commentary on the Bible*, ed. Charles M. Laymon (Nashville, TN: Abingdon, 1971), 1030-1.

2. Matthew 5:39, 44 (NRSV)

In its universal appeal, the early Christian church took seriously the words of Paul's letter to the Galatians:

> For in Christ Jesus you are all children of God through faith. As many of you as were baptized into Christ have clothed yourselves with Christ. There is no longer Jew or Greek, there is no longer slave or free, there is no longer male and female; for all of you are one in Christ Jesus.[3]

The power of these words has been lost to a democratically minded, postmodern world. This was an incredibly radical statement which by itself could have gotten the Apostle Paul executed in the stratified, patristic, Roman society. Yet he saw the new faith of Jesus as a unifying leveler, a shout in the dark for the oneness of humankind. The Early Church shared this vision and was often castigated by pagan commentators for its radical, leveling tendencies, which made princes and paupers equal before this new God preached by Jesus. The faith which would occupy thrones began by telling the world that thrones do not matter, only consciousness does.

The question, yet to be settled, was just how should the burgeoning new faith relate to a pagan society which did not share its worldview? Open revolt was foolish and futile, as the sad experience of Simon bar Kocheba had shown. Besides, Christianity had a strongly anti-militant tone in its early days, reflective of the teachings given by Jesus. Two courses seemed open to second century Christianity: either withdraw from contact with classical civilization or somehow find a bridge between Christian concepts and the best of Greek thought. Quite a few church fathers opted for the former. After all, wasn't Rome the great Antichrist pictured by John in Revelation, drunk on the blood of the saints? Didn't the Roman emperor seduce the world to idolatry through its loyalty oath, which required Emperor worship? What could the church learn from Aristotle? *"What has Athens to do with Jerusalem?"* Tertullian had asked, then launched a diatribe against pagan society which ended with these immortal words:

> We are but of yesterday, and we have filled every place among you—cities, islands, fortresses, towns, market-places, the very

---

3.   Galatians 3:27-28

camps, tribes, companies, palace, Senate, and Forum. We have left you only the temples.[4]

Tertullian was proto-orthodox at this phase of his career, although he would later join a charismatic sect, then reject all sects to form his own heretical group of Tertulianists, which is why St. Tertullian churches are hard to find today. In the mêlée of Early Christian thought, widely divergent communities dueled with words to establish themselves as the One True Church. Although they disagreed vehemently with each other there was one point on which many found agreement: there would be no compromise with paganism, no link between secular learning and the divine revelation of the Church. One was of God, the other of the devil. One would prevail, the other would be swept aside in the Judgment Day soon to come.

Down the coast of North Africa an Alexandrian Christian scholar battled for his understanding of the ancient faith, too. But his theology was not the fierce anti-classicism and intellectual isolationism of Tertullian, it was the first fully developed Christian universalism of Origen the classicist.

Towering, Prolific Genius

Origen was an awesome figure in the early church, a brilliant, passionate, disciplined man. A compulsive writer and incessant lecturer, his influence is felt to this day in doctrines and concepts of even the most orthodox churches, where he was condemned a heretic and has remained so for seventeen hundred years. Origen was a unique personality in world history, a man whose writings ranged far and wide in an encyclopedic scan of human knowledge. Treasures, from a man who was pronounced anathema by church councils soon after his death. Great scholarship and ideas which set the tone for theology in all the generations to come, yet he was branded a heretic.

It is his alleged heresies which make Origen such an interesting person in church history, because a large branch of the Christian tree has held throughout the centuries that Origen was right and the so-called orthodox fathers were wrong. So pervasive is the influence of this early Christian heretic that modern scholars like Catholic theologian Hans Urs Von Balthasar can write,

---

4.   Tertullian, *Apologeticus Adversus Gentes pro Christianis*, MSL, 1:525.

"I know members of religious orders who are praying for the canonization of this martyr and spiritual father of so many saints."[5]

If Origen's ideas had prevailed in the history of the Early Church, a much different form of orthodoxy might have emerged. After all, as previously discussed, orthodoxy is just the majority view; it is not necessarily identical with Truth. It was the "orthodox" who stoned the prophets and crucified Jesus. When reading about Origen, what leaps out of the commentaries and histories of the church are words like *brilliant, genius,* and *towering intellectual giant.* One modern theologian called Origen the Leonardo DaVinci of Early Christianity, so vast in scope were his enterprises.

Even Origen's longstanding foes have grudgingly admitted he was the most brilliant mind of the patristic era, perhaps the keenest intellect in the entire history of Christianity. Standing among such monumental personages as Augustine, Aquinas, and Luther that is indeed quite a compliment. Yet, Origen's brainpower alone hardly would have left such a deep mark on the church had not his intellect been matched by a tremendous, productive scholarship and a passionate personal piety, a piety that would reach excesses in its quest for ascetic purity.

His creativity was boundless. He wrote a mountain of books, so many that even a hardy soul like St. Jerome groaned, "Has anyone read everything that Origen wrote?"[6] Origen's biblical commentaries alone are so vast that none has survived in its entirety. Jerome claims that Origen wrote six thousand books, a number no doubt inflated by ancient exuberance. However, even applying a decimal point to compensate for Jerome's enthusiasm would still leave Origen with six hundred books to his credit, an accomplishment unmatched by any other author in Christian history.

In his unbridled passion for learning, Origen became the first true biblical scholar of the Christian heritage. He learned Hebrew so he could study the Jewish Scriptures in their original language, and tradition says he discoursed at length with learned rabbis about the meanings of Hebrew words and phrases. According to one of his pupils, church historian Eusebius, Origen even found some ancient biblical manuscripts in a jar at Jericho. Thus, in a way, he prefigured modern biblical archaeology and the discovery of the Dead Sea scrolls and the Nag Hammadi Gnostic library.

---

5.   Han Urs Von Balthasar, Preface to *Origen*, ed. Rowan A. Greer, (New York: Paulist Press, 1979), xii.

6.   Johnson, 58.

But not all of Origen's disciplines are admirable to the modern mind. He was also a strict ascetic, devoted to spiritual growth through abusive self-discipline and denying the body its natural desires. He slept on the floor, ate no meat, drank no wine, had only one coat and no shoes. When Origen was seventeen, he urged his father to accept martyrdom, avoiding that fate himself only because his mother hid the young boy's clothes and wouldn't let him out of the house.

Today, his behavior seems obsessive-compulsive: Origen worked far into the night, denied himself all but the scantest sleep, and almost surely castrated himself to remove from his life any sexual temptation and the merest hint of scandal (a practice which fortunately never caught on among theological scholars and authors). He died in C.E. 250 after imprisonment and extensive torture for the crime of professing Christianity. Even Origen's torturers marveled at how heroically he endured this last ordeal. They released him, but he died soon afterward. He was sixty-six.[7]

A Fresh Look at Asceticism, Post-9/11

The first edition of this work contained the following observations:

> It is difficult for twentieth century men and women to comprehend the forces which motivated the ascetics of early Christianity. Some went into the desert to live atop pillars for the rest of their lives; others held their arms upraised in penance for some imagined sin until the joints froze in place. Men whipped themselves with cords, mutilated themselves, and fasted to the edge of death. In this fanatical environment, Origen was almost a moderate.

Sadly, the overall theme of this paragraph—that readers today cannot possibly conceive of religious fanaticism which reaches such a life-denigrating magnitude—is no longer true for twenty-first century men and women. The post 9/11 world has now begun to comprehend how a xenophobic religious faith, which avoids the counter-balance gained through dialogue with other worldviews, can mutate from impassioned devotion, to self-righteous zeal, to self-destructive extremism, to suicidal antagonism toward anyone who sees the world differently.

---

7.   *Ibid.*

Now people look at the images of passenger jets smashing into buildings, and at some level they understand this affront to moral values was a religious act for the terrorists, a pseudo-holy ritual of suicide-homicide, driven by forces not unlike the demons populating the minds of ascetics through history. Although their degree of fanaticism may be similar, the significant difference between modern religio-terrorists and religious ascetics throughout history is that the life-denying exercises of those self-flagellating wretches have usually been directed at themselves and seldom brutalized or killed other people.

Misguided religionists who starve, torture, or immolate themselves may claim some kind of imaginary martyrdom, but those who murder innocents in fulfillment of a death wish have no standing to fantasize their suicide was a sacramental act. Although the 9/11 terrorists died with shouts of *"God is Great!"* on their lips, it is possible to imagine the Lord could not hear their cries, because God was crying.

Origen's Vision

Whatever mental demons drove Origen to disfigurement and denial of the good of this world, his asceticism never involved harming other people and it is not reflected in his writing, which flows with coolheaded logic and a vision of the faith motivated by deep love for God. And what was that vision? Rowan A. Greer of Yale Divinity School described Origen's great hope, the historical/mystical dream he had for the faith of Jesus:

> Specifically, he saw the Christian hope not as an alternative to the Roman world, but as the catalyst that could rescue and transform what was best in it. His theology was an attempt to translate the Gospel into a language intelligible to the pagan, especially the thoughtful and educated pagan.[8]

Origen's passion for this vision—his hope that Jesus Christ could save Hellenistic culture from decay and ruin—drove him beyond moderation to asceticism and eventually to death as a martyr. For him Christianity was not merely the Truth, it was the only hope for a world disintegrating before his eyes. The contribution Origen made to Western thought is unparalleled in world history. He became the first fully competent philosopher/theologian to think

---

8. Rowan A. Greer, (ed.), *Origen* (NY: Paulist Press, 1979), 2.

through the Christian teachings and devise a systematic theology that spoke to the mind as well as the heart. In doing so he unintentionally provoked a controversy which still rages in Christendom, although the passing centuries have rendered the Origenist position triumphant in Christian theological circles of higher thought.

Three ideas are worthy of considering in specific details: his *Christology*, or theology of the nature and person of Jesus; his *universalism*, concept of universal salvation; and his use of *allegory* to interpret the Bible after the manner of the Stoics and pioneered by Philo Judaeus. In all three categories, this Early Church genius and father of Christian universalism qualifies as a long-lost relative to modern Metaphysical Christianity. Origen himself would have approved of an open-minded approach to his works. He wrote: "If anyone can find something better and can confirm what he says by clear proofs from Holy Scripture, let his opinion be preferred to ours."[9]

Christology

Origen believed Jesus of Nazareth was the earthly manifestation of the *Divine Mind* or *Logos*. He saw Jesus Christ as *preexistent*, i.e., having lived before incarnation in this world as Jesus of Nazareth. For Origen, Jesus was a being of impeccable character and spirituality whom Divine Mind chose for the mission of bringing salvation to all God's children. Origen believed Jesus was so thoroughly in harmony with God that to see Jesus was to know what God was like. In this regard, Origen foreshadowed twentieth century thinkers of the neo-orthodox school, such as Swiss theologian Karl Barth.

In Volume One of his classic series on *A History of Christian Thought*, Arthur Cushman McGiffert described Origen's Christology:

> The divine Logos could not directly assume a human body, the unlikeness between them being too great. He therefore united with one of the created spirits who by his preeminent virtue had proved himself worthy of the honor. This spirit, joined to the divine Logos, took on a human body, thus becoming a human soul, and advanced step by step until he attained complete divinity.[10]

---

9.   Arthur Cushman McGiffert, A History of Christian Thought, Vol. I (NY: Charles Scribner's Sons, 1932), 229.
10.   *Ibid.*, 225-226.

For Origen, Christ consciousness was attained, not ordained. Although his mythology of a preexistent match between a human soul and the Divine Mind may not reflect the beliefs of modern metaphysical Christians, Origen was a freethinker who paved the way for the belief in preexistence, reincarnation and Christ consciousness. When Origen was condemned, it was his belief in pre-existence of souls which church councils stiffly pronounced *anathema* or accursed. This closed the door to a belief in reincarnation also, since preexistence of a soul is logically required for that soul to reincarnate in this world.

Origen also leaned toward the Fillmorean definition of the trinity as *mind, idea,* and *expression,* although he never expressed it exactly this way. He held that the Father is eternally generating the Son, and that all created souls are in some mystical way one with this one Power. Origen goes as far as saying that the Logos is the Father in the same way that a thought represents its thinker: Mind and idea are somehow one. It would take metaphysicians centuries to sort this out, but Origen held a beacon in the darkness by which many mystics to come would find their way.

Universalism: Hell is Dead

Universalism was Origen's belief that all would be saved. He was unequivocal on this, insisting that any belief in eternal punishment was unworthy of the God of Jesus. Origen repeatedly insisted that the "wrath of God" is not some emotional outburst on the part of Divine Mind, but a series of natural consequences and built-in "punishments" which teach, purify, and uplift the soul in its quest for holiness. He was certain that terms like *heaven, hell, resurrection,* and the *Second* Coming had symbolic meanings that far transcended any crude literalism. He taught that everyone would be saved because God is not demented, and it would take a demented deity to punish anyone for all eternity. When his opponents fired back that his theology could mean that even the devil would be saved, Origen agreed. Everyone will be reconciled with God, bar none. Universalism means even any supernatural beings temporarily employed as demons will return to the Father.

Although demonology receives little mention in today's theology, universalism has triumphed. Only the conservative fringe of Christianity still clings to the charred edges of hell in a vain attempt to convince people that a fiery afterlife awaits evil-doers. The idea of eternal punishment is considered so repugnant to the modern mind, so immoral and sub-Christian, that it has been summarily dismissed from the discussions of religious scholars.

However, the general population remains unaware of Origen's triumph because church leaders on the Religious Right make a lot more noise than the moderate center-left majority. Consequently, the conservatives have succeeded in convincing the public that '*turn-or-burn*' is not only prevalent but the only authentic Christian doctrine. Nothing could be further from the truth. Anglican theologian John Macquarrie, who at the time held the prestigious academic chair known as the Lady Margaret Professorship of Theology at Oxford University, pronounced the following *anathema* a generation ago:

> Needless to say, we utterly reject the idea of a hell where God everlastingly punishes the wicked, without hope of deliverance. Even earthly penologists are more enlightened nowadays. Rather we must believe that God will never cease from his quest for universal reconciliation, and we can firmly hope for his victory in this quest, through recognizing that this victory can only come when at last there is the free cooperation of every responsible creature.[11]

From this brief quote it is patently obvious the debate is over. Writing in the early 1970's, this Church of England scholar could barely contain his distaste for the doctrine of eternal damnation. Origen's sensible point of view has prevailed. Hell is dead.

Allegory

Allegory was Origen's mystical interpretation of biblical symbolism. Origen held that there is a threefold meaning in Scripture that corresponds to the threefold division he saw in human nature: body, soul, and spirit, which equates to literal, moral, and spiritual. George W. Anderson describes Origen's biblical interpretation:

> The literal sense is what is understood by the ordinary, unenlightened Christian. The higher senses, the moral and spiritual, are appropriate to those further advanced in understanding and insight,

---

11. John Macquarrie, *twentieth century Religious Thought* (London: SCM Press, 1971), p.357.

though none can fathom the ultimate divine mystery concealed in scripture.[12]

Is literalism valid? Yes, Origen said grudgingly, it is valid for those at that level of understanding. But absurdity will not pass as history, even if the Bible says so. When the book of Genesis allows three "days" to pass before God creates the sun, any sensible person can see Genesis cannot be taken literally without descending into illogic. In the creation account readers are encountering either fiction or metaphor. Anderson continues:

> (Origen believed)…such difficult or offensive elements in the text were put there by God to incite the reader to search for the higher meanings. The moral sense is related not only to duty and obedience but to the entire range of the soul's experience. The spiritual sense conveys the divine nature and purpose.[13]

Here Origen is reaching for a way to release deeper meanings from the treasure house of the Scriptures. Following in Philo's footsteps, he is a true son of the Alexandrian school of biblical interpretation, grounded in allegorical and mystical methods rather than enslaved to the literal. Where Tertullian will cry, "I believe it because it is absurd!" Origen will shake his head and sigh, "We must see whether it is not possible to find a more worthy interpretation for these passages."[14]

Writing as he did on the eve of the fall of Rome, Origen's work is a vast series of affirmations, in theological language, proclaiming the goodness of God and the perfectibility of humanity. When voices were being raised within Christianity to wall off Christian thought from the rest of human experience, Origen sounded his trumpet call for universalism in thought and deed. He believed in the capacity of humanity, his brothers and sisters throughout humanity's ages to come, to find Truth through following the indwelling spirit

---

12. George W. Anderson, "The History of Biblical Interpretation," *The Interpreter's One Volume Commentary on the Bible*, ed. Charles M. Laymon (Nashville, TN: Abingdon, 1971), 973.
13. *Ibid.*
14. Origen, *On First Principles*, ed. Rowan A. Greer, (NY: Paulist Press, 1979), 196.

of Truth. Clearly, his words ring down the corridors of time as though he were writing for today:

> We see, therefore, that men have a blood kinship with God…it is possible that a rational mind also, by advancing from a knowledge of small to a knowledge of greater things and from things visible to things invisible, may attain to an increasingly perfect understanding.[15]

Origen has been widely proclaimed a great genius of the early church. In much of his teaching, he was a direct predecessor to modern Metaphysical Christianity. Why, then, did a dark cloud loom over the sunny optimism of the early church? What kept the Origenists from spreading the good news of universal salvation to the ends of the earth and replaced their optimism with the bad news of human sinfulness, which would linger into the twentieth century? This study now turns its attention to the process by which the Church became purveyors of a fall-and-redemption model based on original sin.

---

15. Origen, *On First Principles*, trans. G. W. Butterworth (New York: Harper Torchbooks, 1966), 327.

3

Free Will or Predestination?

Pelagius, Augustine, and Hypatia
(Fifth Century C.E.)

The fifth century of the Christian Era saw one age ending and another beginning. Ancient civilization, the world of classical Greek creativity and impetuous curiosity, collapsed and died of old age, while the medieval period, shrouded in superstition and cowed by fears of hellfire, was just being born. It was a transition period for western civilization, a bottleneck between two worlds, much like today. As with any turbulent period, contrasting prevalent forces pulled at fifth century people from several directions at once, creating tremendous tension at the center of life. It was the sort of age William Butler Yeats described, when…

> Things fall apart; the center cannot hold;
> Mere anarchy is loosed upon the world,
> The blood-dimmed tide is loosed, and everywhere The ceremony of
> innocence is drowned.
> The best lack all conviction,
> while the worst are full of passionate intensity.[1]

Leaders of the Church were not exempt from this furious commotion. Except now Christianity was no longer a persecuted minority but presided as

---

1. William Butler Yeats, Untitled Poem, *Origen,* ed. Rowan A. Greer
    (NY: Paulist Press, 1979), 1-2.

29

the only lawful religious faith of the Empire. Paganism maintained its hold on the people only in the countryside surrounding the great cities where rural folk clung to ancestral traditions, some for the comfort afforded by the round of season-based agrarian rituals, others for fear of new ideas. In fact, the word *pagan* comes from the Latin *paganus,* or "country-dweller."

However, in the centers of Hellenistic civilization, the triumph of Jesus over Jove was complete. Or was it?

Persecuting The Pagans

Certainly, the official religion of the Roman world was now the Christian faith. But Church leaders began to adopt the very practices which they had reviled in their pagan counterparts a generation ago. After centuries of sporadic persecutions, one would expect the leaders of Christianity to understand the needs of the oppressed and allow for religious tolerance within the crumbling remains of Roman civilization now that the Church was supreme. They did not.

When Christian orthodoxy became the only lawful religion of the Empire, the formerly persecuted sect busily set to work persecuting, harassing, and killing the pagans and, even more incredibly, persecuting other Christians who failed to pass the orthodox sniff test. Although weakened by war and internal decay, Rome was still strong enough to torture her own people for cultural nonconformity, but now orthodox Christians held the whips and drove pagans and heretics into hiding. It was a sad departure from the spirit of ancient Christianity and the inclusive teachings of Jesus Christ.

Medieval Christianity would become a patchwork of church fiefdoms where isolated intellectuals secluded themselves to rethink the message of Jesus while the rank-and-file Christians were held in spiritual serfdom to a system of religious and political oppression that controlled life in this world and the world to come. Every age has produced its great thinkers, and medieval Europe was no exception, as shall become apparent when this survey moves on to study people like John Scotus Erigena and Meister Eckhart. In fact, it is the perennial task of theology to rethink and reshape the Christian message for each succeeding generation.

Historian Paul Johnson reiterates the crucial observation which has been made repeatedly in this study of Christian history, i.e., from day one when Jesus gathered his disciples there has *never* been anything approaching universal agreement on what the Christian faith teaches. Sects, schisms, and new thought movements have grudgingly co-existed from the very beginnings of the faith. Any of these could have captured the "orthodox" position and become a central belief of Christianity.[2] Most, however, remained a part of the harmony of the church rather than becoming the melody line.

Early in the fifth century, two tunes vied for the melody line in the developing medieval symphony. The one that emerged victorious was a sad tune, indeed. It told of the evil nature of humankind, the need for hellfire to keep the unruly passions of unregenerate man in his place. It sang of salvation, but only for the few, the Elect, and it chanted somber tones about the total inability of humans to do anything of value because of the total depravity which characterizes Adam's descendents, born in original sin.

For the majority of medieval Christian thinkers, everything human was corrupt; the natural state of human consciousness was full rebellion against God. The natural destination for all humankind is a quick flight through life toward a richly merited damnation. At the end of life, Jesus waits, sometimes painted above a rainbow with a sword coming out of one ear and a lily out of the other. Jesus judges the soul according to a preordained, predestined roster of the saved and the damned. A few chosen souls wing their way to eternal bliss in heaven, but the vast majority of human spirits fall into the abyss to be tortured with Satan for all eternity.

The Real "Heresiarch"?

This was the worldview of the medieval church. It was Christianity at its least healthy expression, one of the most pessimistic, pathological theologies this world has ever produced. Yet, orthodoxy didn't have to go the way it did. Johnson comments:

> The story might have been different. There were elements in Christianity at the beginning of the fifth century striving to create a distinctive Christian higher culture on Origenist lines. Their frustration and destruction was very largely the work of one man...Augustine was the dark genius of imperial Christianity, the ideologue of the Church-State alliance, and the fabricator of the medieval mentality.[3]

---

2. Johnson, 86.
3. Ibid.

These "elements in Christianity…striving to create a distinctive Christian higher culture on Origenist lines" rallied around a most unlikely controversialist. A pious soul who loved the Church and despised discord, a moderate ascetic who believed love and reason would carry Truth to victory, the British monk Pelagius was ill-suited for his task as leader of a church-splitting insurrectionist. That role would await centuries for the defiant genius of a Martin Luther.

Despite his conciliatory nature, Pelagius has been called the *heresiarch*, or father of heresy. A fresh look at the issues might show otherwise. Johnson again:

> Certainly, if we contrast his philosophy with Paul's, it can be seen that Augustine, not Pelagius, was the heresiarch—the greatest of them all in terms of his influence.[4]

However, theologian Matthew Fox, himself a vocal critic of Augustinian theology, says European Christianity tended to exacerbate Augustine's negative attitude about human character:

> Original sin is an idea that Augustine developed late in his life and, to his credit, it was not all that significant in his theology either. Sad to say, however, original sin grew to become the starting point for Western religion's flight from nature, creation, and the God of creation.[5]

Do Humans Have the Power to Choose?

Augustine fought for a dark vision of humanity, a gloomy gospel, pessimistic and predestinarian, flying like a storm flag above a world gripped by sin. Pelagius wanted a beach umbrella—a sunny, optimistic theology, shaped by free will and brimming with human potential. The combatants formed their battle lines along the ridgelines of opposing answers to three strategic questions. The whole structure of moral theology—fundamental ideas on the nature of humanity, like original sin, Divine Election and irresistible grace—hangs upon the way an individual answers these few inquires.

---

4.   *Ibid.,* 112.
5.   Matthew Fox, *Original Blessing* (NY: Tarcher/Penguin, 2000), 49.

1. Is human nature essentially good?

2. Are people free to choose their own destinies, or predestined to either salvation or damnation?

3. Most importantly, does a person have the power to do good without God forcing the deed upon him?

To all of the above, Augustine said, *"No!"* Pelagius said, *"Yes!"* The issue was clear-cut and unmistakable.

Their dispute began with the basics. Pelagius was concerned with morality and ethics. He saw Augustine's emphasis on the inability of depraved humanity to do anything good as an excuse to avoid moral responsibility. If a person cannot act morally, if keeping God's rules is beyond human ability, why should anyone struggle to be a good person? If humanity is predestined to heaven or hell, what difference does it make how people treat their neighbors in the here and now? The monstrous absurdity that God damns and blesses whomsoever He chooses, regardless of their efforts or character, seemed subhuman to Pelagius, let alone sub-Christian. He reasoned that humans must be able to do good or the whole concept of good and evil is useless.

Coelsestrius, one of his strongest supporters, condensed the Pelagian argument in a brilliant display of classical logic:

> Again, it is to be inquired whether a man ought to be sinless. Without a doubt, he ought. And if a man ought, he can; if he cannot he ought not. And if a man ought not be sinless then he ought to be sinful, and that will not be sin which it is admitted he ought to do.[6]

Flawed or Free?

Augustine was not impressed. For him, there was ample evidence in the world for his belief in total depravity and preordained damnation/salvation. Physical death and suffering were but two examples of divine retribution visited upon all humanity for the sin of Adam. Augustine believed people are born in original sin, which he unhesitatingly identified with the act of sexual reproduction.

---

6. *Johnson.,* 122.

All humanity is fatally flawed because when Adam sinned the human race fell from grace to total rebellion against God, hence death, suffering, sickness, and pain.

Pelagius replied that death is natural, not the result of the fall of Adam. Death is a result of being born finite and would have happened anyway, he said, even if Adam had not sinned. All humans have free choice, just as Adam did. Anything less would be unworthy of the Creator and Father of Jesus Christ, the God of love and justice.[7]

Augustine and the medieval church after him insisted that humans sin because their basic nature is corrupt: people sin because they are sinners. Pelagius countered that human nature is neither wholly corrupt nor wholly perfect, yet it is free. Freedom means the ability to choose good or evil; it means that total depravity is nonsense, and spiritual perfection comes a bit later in the program. Pelagius turned the Augustinian formula around: people are *sinners* because they *sin*. People are imperfect because they are still working on their perfection.

For Pelagius and the Pelagians, people are not born thieves but become thieves by stealing, which is an act of free choice. And, he reasoned, if it is a free choice to sin then humans must be free to be perfect, too. Pelagius admitted that perfection was rare, but insisted it was possible. Is this were not so, he asked, what did Jesus mean when He commanded: "…be perfect, as your heavenly father is perfect"?[8]

At first Augustine and his party, which included the brilliant but disparaging Saint Jerome, treated Pelagius with utmost respect. Well known as a pious, erudite soul whose character was above reproach, Augustine initially seemed a bit embarrassed that he had differences of opinion with Pelagius. As late as 413 C.E., Augustine sent the British monk, who then resided at Rome, a courteous epistle. The real break between them occurred a year later. It was prompted by an event so trivial that history only knows of it because the incident became a pivotal point in the Pelagian Controversy.

Demetrias, daughter of a wealthy Roman gentleman, decided to take the veil as a virgin, the early Christian term for the female religious vocation now called *nuns*. She was living at Carthage when she embarked on this new voca-

---

7.   Arthur Cushman McGiffert, A *History* of *Christian Thought, Vol. II* (NY: Charles Scribner's Sons, 1933), 128.

8.   Matthew 5:48, RSV.

tion, but her Roman mother wanted the event celebrated throughout the Empire. She solicited and received lengthy essays of advice for her daughter from well-known contemporary divines, among them Jerome and Pelagius.

Jerome got a copy of Pelagius' letter and was so outraged he brought it to the attention of his friend, the Bishop of Hippo, Augustine. Augustine read the letter, agreeing with Jerome's evaluation. In fact, he thought the treatise so dangerous he felt compelled to warn the mother of Demetrias about its doubtful orthodoxy.[9]

Human Nature: Bad or Good?

The letter, which may seem innocent enough today, nevertheless contained the following passage which infuriated Augustine:

> Whenever I have to speak concerning moral instruction and holy living I am accustomed to point out first the force and quality of human nature and what it is able to accomplish and then to incite the mind of the hearer to many kinds of virtue, since it is not without profit to be summoned to those things which perhaps he had assumed are impossible to him. For we are by no means able to tread the way of virtue unless we have hope as a companion.[10]

This seemingly innocuous exhortation to virtuous living angered Augustine because he considered it sacrilegious to speak of human nature as able to accomplish anything. Jerome, best known for his translation of the Bible into the Latin Vulgate, called Pelagius a "corpulent dog," shouting that Pelagianism was a dangerous heresy.

Yet, Pelagius was acquitted by a synod of Palestinian bishops in 415 C.E. His position was by far more popular than the pessimism of the North Africans under the lead of Augustine. Pelagianism was not only popular, it was an ancient viewpoint, as Johnson indicates:

> Pelagius was not an isolate heretic. He represented the ordinary doctrine of people who were educated in Greek thinking, especially in

---

9.   Johnson, 229.
10. McGiffert, 125-126.

Stoic traditions, and for whom freedom is the essential nature of man.[11]

Essential Difference: Anthropology

Despite its long history as a minority branch on the church family tree, New Thought Christianity today shares much in common with mainstream theology, especially in its post-modern expression. Previously controversial views on God as Absolute Good and the nonexistence of hell face little opposition in academic theology today. Although views which emphasize somewhat different interpretations of the "good news" than other Protestants, New Thought ministers and teachers can quite comfortably study Bible, theology and pastoral care at theological seminaries run by United Methodists, Evangelical Lutherans, Christian Church Disciples, Presbyterians, Episcopalians, UCC's and assorted Congregationalists, and other denominations. Ministers, priests and nuns frequently speak at New Thought churches about spirituality, and some Metaphysical Christians have discovered deeper realms of Spirit through private encounters with God amid the tranquil, spiritually conducive surroundings of Catholic monasteries and Protestant retreat centers.

New Thought Christianity differs from the vast majority of its brothers and sisters in the progressive wing of the Christian faith over some issues, but not about Jesus or God or Scripture. Support for metaphysical beliefs can be found in the work of various established theologians. The point at which New Thought and progressive Christianity part company occurs when the discussion turns to *anthropology*, which in theological language refers to the "doctrine of man" (i.e., human nature). New Thought is Pelagian; most other Christians are Augustinian.

To summarize: The anthropological foundation of most Christian theology sees humanity existing in a state of brokenness, separated from the Creator by an infinite gulf, and the dysfunction has a metaphysical basis. Humanity is part of the problem and cannot find the answer within itself. Augustine's grim pessimism has carried the day so completely that the idea of innate human goodness is not seriously discussed, let alone defended. Even a movement as steadfastly liberal as Unitarian-Universalism, which is so anti-traditionalist it refuses to call itself a Christian denomination, nevertheless tends to portray

---

11. Johnson, 123.

humanity as fatally flawed. The concern about sin for Christian progressives does not center on individual acts—he or she sinned by doing this or that. Corporate states of being—for example, poverty, war, homophobia, and institutional racism—are examples of sin for liberal religionists. Conservative Christianity sees sin as a *verb*, something people do; liberal Christianity tends to consider sin a *noun*, identifying conditions in society at large. This sweeping generalization doubtless will not survive close examination, but perhaps the contours of truth are discernible in the haze of oversimplification.

Radical Freedom

While both conservative and liberal Christians tend to see humanity through Augustinian lenses, Metaphysical Christianity is thoroughly Pelagian, finding more reason for optimism in human nature than the widely held pessimism in the general population. However, mainline and Metaphysical churches agree upon one point, i.e., people are free to choose their destinies. Considering this presumptive free will, a New Thought Christian might ask, "If, as Augustine insisted, God alone has the freedom to act, doesn't the very fact of human ability to 'choose' authenticate our divine nature?" It certainly fits everyday experience. People choose to accept or reject their highest good. And here's a thought to ponder the next time someone laments human weakness: people can choose to turn away from the good, something which God cannot do. Humans experience life in this world as an adventure of radical freedom.

One could argue, with some degree of cogency, that God does not provide the answers to great questions of life without requiring effort on the part of the individual. Look at the history of homo sapiens. Humanity is always struggling upward, blundering, and finding its way again. Humans had to discover fire, then how to make fire and control the flame, then animal husbandry, agriculture, and so on. The Prometheus myth notwithstanding, there is no archeological evidence that exalted beings from on high revealed these techniques to humanity, regardless of the tales developed later to explain the miracles of discovery. Contrary to Augustine, history suggests that humans are not so much fatally flawed as they are temporarily undeveloped. If Pelagius had triumphed, perhaps a more positive attitude might have resulted, which could have produced an earlier array of beneficial discoveries without so many centuries of intervening disease, pain and toil.

Bribe Thy Neighbor...

Augustine would not relent. He hounded Pelagius and his followers across the length of the Empire. He had them twice declared heretical at synods in North Africa. He wrote volumes against Pelagianism. Finally, he was able to get the whole affair before the Bishop of Rome, Pope Zosimus. At first the Holy See inclined toward Pelagius, who had the support of several rich and powerful Roman families. The African faction pressed for Pelagianism to be declared heretical. Zosimus wavered, hesitated. He clearly did not want to rule on this. With so many influential people on both sides, he was bound to infuriate someone, and perhaps even provoke a major split in the church. Paul Johnson says the North Africans grew impatient. Finally, Augustine's party resorted to outright bribery:

> Eighty fine Numidian stallions, bred on episcopal estates in Africa, were shipped to Italy and distributed among the imperial cavalry commanders whose squadrons, in the last resort, imposed Augustine's theory of grace. To the imperial authorities, the Pelagians were represented as disturbers of the public peace.[12]

What theology could not accomplish by argument, imperial power imposed through force of arms cajoled by bribery. Zosimus reluctantly issued a formal condemnation of Pelagius in 418 C.E. It was a sad commentary on the direction the so-called orthodox church was taking.

"Capitur urbs quae totum cepit orbem."

Yet, it was not by the force of his personality alone, nor by the machinations of his political allies, that Augustine defeated the optimistic Pelagians. Just as the clouds of controversy gathered, an event occurred which overshadowed all other happenings in fifth century Europe. It was a calamity so profound that Augustine's developing theory of human total depravity finally made sense when seen in the light of this earth-shattering cataclysm.

In 411 C.E., Alaric the Goth shocked the Hellenistic world by capturing and sacking the city of Rome. The eternal city, which Tertullian had believed

---

12. *Ibid.,* 120.

would last until Judgment Day, had fallen. In far-off Bethlehem, Saint Jerome pushed aside his translation of the Latin Bible to cry in anguish:

> The entire human race is implicated in the catastrophe. My voice is choked, and my words are broken with sobs while I write: *"Capitur urbs quae totum cepit orbem."* (The city is now taken that once held the world.)[13]

Augustine watched these events in the momentary safety of North Africa. Even though he could not know that his own region would soon fall to barbarian invasions and he would die in the siege of Hippo, Augustine was troubled, too. Could there be any better evidence that his position was the true one—man was evil, corrupt, totally depraved—than this world-toppling event? He took paper and pen and wrote: "The city of God endureth forever, though the greatest city on earth is fallen...."[14]

Rome, he decided, was the city of man, whose transitory efforts would always be tainted by sin. The Church, on the other hand, was the *City of God*, a divine kingdom which would neither fall nor fail. It was these events which prompted him to write his greatest work by that title. He hammered away at this theme for the rest of his life, and in a world where the foundations shook and people cried for some sort of stability, indeed this was a comforting theme. Perhaps more than anything, the fall of Rome sealed the doom of Pelagian optimism and opened the dark doorway to medieval oppression, fear, and pessimism. With that element dominating human consciousness, the advent of the Dark Ages was assured.

Hypatia of Alexandria

Suddenly, everything from classical civilization became suspect, for did it not represent the city of man, the kingdom of Satan? One case, which sadly showed this gathering gloom, was Hypatia of Alexandria. Even in the city of Philo and Origen, that bastion of ancient liberalism, reactionary forces grew strong in the fifth century. Fanaticism moved quickly to attack anyone with classical learning, which included people like Hypatia.

---

13. Robert Payne, *The Horizon Book* of *Ancient Rome* (NY: American Heritage, 1966), 366.
14. *Ibid.*

She was an extraordinary woman. A contemporary account of her accomplishments has survived, written by the Christian historian Socrates. Hypatia was a brilliant scholar with credentials in literature and the sciences. She was the curator of the great classical museum of Alexandria, a research and teaching facility unmatched in the ancient world. Daughter of the philosopher Theon, Hypatia was reputed to be the finest philosopher of her time. As a Platonist, she fell into the general school of thought which informed Philo, Clement, Origen, and other "fathers" of the ancient faith, although she was not a Christian. That, more than anything, was her great crime in the eyes of the fanatical street rabble of Alexandria who claimed to be followers of Jesus. Historian Socrates writes of Hypatia:

> She explained all the principles of philosophy to her auditors. Therefore many from all sides, wishing to study philosophy, came to her. On account of the self-possession and ease of manner which she had acquired by her study, she not infrequently appeared with modesty in the presence of magistrates. Neither did she feel abashed in entering an assembly of men. For all men, on account of her extraordinary dignity and virtue, admired her all the more.[15]

Martyr to Classical Civilization

By all reports, Hypatia was a superior person. Another time in history she might have been celebrated and remembered for her academic and philosophical achievements and her high character. Instead, she would be a martyr to the demise of classical civilization. In 415 C.E. a fanatical mob, stirred by Saint Cyril the local bishop, waylaid her on the way home. Socrates tells the unpleasant story:

> Dragging her from her carriage they took her to the church called Caesareum. There they completely stripped her and murdered her with tiles...This affair brought no little opprobrium (disgrace), not only upon Cyril but upon the whole Alexandrian Church.[16]

---

15. Joseph Cullen Ayer, Jr., *A Source Book for Ancient Church History* (NY: Charles Scribner's Sons, 1913), 373.
16. *Ibid.*, 373-374.

Historian Socrates expressed horror at this act, which was to become painfully frequent as medieval fears and heresy-hunting took the place of early Christian enthusiasm and universalism. "And surely murders, fights, and actions of that sort are altogether alien to those who hold the things of Christ."[17] Instead of a celebrated figure in philosophy, Hypatia's fate was to become a martyr to classical learning. Augustine himself provided the rationale for state persecution and torture of heretics.

One cannot help but wonder what might have been the course of Western civilization if Pelagius, not Augustine, had prevailed. Perhaps the world was not ready yet for Pelagianism. Perhaps human consciousness was not at a level to accept responsibility for its actions in an atmosphere of freedom. Perhaps the people of that long-dead era were like frightened children playing at the edge of night, terrorized by the shapes of shadows and not knowing how to find the light switch that would turn darkness to day, even though Jesus had told them, *"You are the light of the world."*

Augustine's Mixed Legacy

Certainly, people like Pelagius and Hypatia are examples of humanity at its best. But even Augustine, who bequeathed a heritage of pessimism, also designated a goal to strive toward. He ardently wished that each believer might come into direct communion with God; his *Confessions*, his spiritual autobiography, so clearly shows this. A child of his age, Augustine never intended that his teachings should lead to the Dark Ages or become the proof-texts for the great terror of the Inquisition. The group consciousness of medieval humanity took it in that direction against his good intent.

Augustine, Pelagius, and Hypatia represented three vastly different worldviews, yet each has contributed to the development of Metaphysical Christianity. It would take centuries for Origen's universalism and Pelagian free will to capture center stage in Christian theology. However, today this is the case. Virtually all modern theologians, outside the fundamentalist fringe, accept Origen's teaching that none shall be damned forever, and Pelagius' insistence on individual free will, albeit with lingering uncertainty about the perfectibility of human character. The victory of Pelagian theology of hope over Augustinian gloom and doom could have come sooner if the church had read and studied its mystical theologians.

---

17. *Ibid.*

The first three studies of the ancestors to practical Christianity have explored the teachings of a few fathers of the faith: Philo, Origen, and Pelagius. Now it is time to turn to the medieval period and look at some "Marvelous Medieval Mystics" by examining the works of a Christian philosopher (John Scotus Erigena) and a preacher/teacher whose mysticism is still popular reading (Meister Eckhart). But first, the task of discovering long-lost ancestors requires digging a little deeper to strike the foundation stone for all medieval and subsequent mystical writings in the Christian culture, the great father of mysticism in the Western world, Dionysius the Areopagite. His influence is enormous, yet few people outside academic circles have heard of this unknown soldier of the faith, whose disentombment is the next goal of this study.

II

Those Marvelous Medieval Mystics

4

Brightness of the Divine Darkness

Pseudo-Dionysius the Areopagite
(c. Fifth Century C.E.)

One of the many surprises students of religious studies will encounter early is that quite a few ancient religious texts are forgeries, even books of the Bible. Large numbers of letters and treatises, which assert themselves to be from the hand of well-known figures, flow from the imagination of unknown authors writing much later under pen names. Paul Tillich said pseudonymous writing was widely practiced in classical civilization.

> What seems to us now a falsification was a custom in ancient writing. It was not a betrayal in any technical or moral sense to launch one's books under famous names.[1]

There is ample evidence that quite a few biblical books were not written by the persons to whom the church has traditionally assigned them. Scholars have known for over a hundred years that Moses could not have written the Torah. (After all, he dies in the last book.) Some Christians are more fascinated than jarred by learning the well-established conclusions of modern scholarship, e.g., that the Gospels were not written by the Apostles and half the letters of Paul were actually written by his disciples years after Paul's martyrdom.[2] Although

---

1. Paul Tillich, *A History of Christian Thought* (NY: Simon & Schuster, 1968), 90.
2. This isn't even controversial in biblical scholarship any more.

clergy who graduate from mainline Protestant and Catholic theological seminaries are well aware of these historic facts, the new paradigm is just beginning to trickle down to the local churches. Even so, the idea of biblical authors working with a pseudonym is so disturbing to conservative Christians that a significant number of otherwise progressive clergy continue to withhold the historical information that their seminary professors taught them a generation ago for fear of alienating the literalists among them. Presbyterian scholar James D. Smart has called this the permission of ignorance.[3]

A cynic might observe that, in the market-driven economy of American religious institutions, where people vote with their feet and their checkbooks, sometimes it is easier to permit ignorance than challenge it. Perhaps a gentler form of prophetic ministry can yet be discovered by which people could learn their histories without the corresponding shock to their worldviews. However, if the past is any indication of the future, biblical literalism will not simply morph into post-modern thought. Most worldviews are not transformed but wholly replaced by the new paradigm. Paganism did not become Christianity, it was replaced by it.

Creative Cauldron

If the practice of pseudonymous writing was so widespread, the natural question is why did so many books get mislabeled? Was it intentional deceit? The answer is *yes and no*. Sometimes the intent was deceitful, sometimes it was not. As previously discussed, Early Christianity was a bubbling, creative cauldron of ideas. Most preaching and teaching came not through written documents but by the spoken word. Sometimes, a teacher would write down his or her thoughts, or the thoughts of a mentor, like Paul, or a companion of Jesus, like Matthew, John or Thomas. These writings often became the only link people had with the generations who had walked with and talked with Jesus and the Apostles.

The written word had special power because it could be repeated and studied, whereas oral speech fades with the memory. Besides, written teaching tends to convey extra power, especially when framed in well-chosen words. Paul frankly admits that his writings are much more effective than his physical presence.[4] Some of Paul's readership apparently believed their task was to find

---

3.   James D. Smart, *The Strange Silence of the Bible in the Church* (Phila.: Westminster Press, 1970), 69.
4.   II Corinthians 10:9-10.

copies of his letters to other churches and read them, too, although they hardly considered his practical lessons had the weight of sacred text.[5]

As this body of Apostolic era writings became more available to church communities in the Second and Third Centuries, some of the new Christian books finally began to find use as Scripture beside the Jewish Bible. As time passed and schools of Christian thought continued to diverge in various communities, it became important that a viewpoint representing one's theology made it into this emerging category of sacred Christian scripture. Often, people who considered themselves followers of major teachers—Paul, James, John, Peter and others—set down ideas they believed their masters would have taught and attributed the Apostolic name to the newer work. They borrowed this method from common practice in Hellenistic civilization.

Hundreds of years before, Plato had done the same. Using his mentor, Socrates, as the main character, Plato wrote his great *Dialogues*. Thus the *Dialogues of Plato* are really the *Dialogues of Socrates*. Or are they? Did Plato write from memories of what Socrates taught, or is Plato invoking the name of his mentor to give authority to his own ideas? As mentioned, several unknown authors wrote in Paul's name so effectively their "Epistles" fooled the wider community and made it into the New Testament canon (Ephesians, I and II Timothy, Titus, and perhaps II Thessalonians and Colossians). Some wrote "According to" the disciples (Matthew, I and II Peter, John). Some never claimed to be the work of an Apostle but were later attributed to a disciple of Jesus by church tradition (Mark, Luke-Acts, Hebrews, James, and Jude).

More surprising for newcomers to church history are the scores of books from the early Christian period (through C.E. 200) that did not make the New Testament canon, yet claimed authorship by the hand of an Apostle or a major figure from the Apostolic age. To name just a few: Gospels by the Apostles Thomas, Peter, Phillip, and Mary, the Gospel of the Ebionites; the Acts of John, Peter, Paul, Andrew, and Thomas; the Teaching of the Apostles (*Didache*); Letters of Pilate, Barnabas, and the Apostles; the Martyrdom of Matthew; the Infancy Gospels—the list goes on.[6] The overwhelming majority of scholars believe these to be well-intended forgeries, often with ulterior

---

5. Colossians 4:16.
6. M. R. James, *The Apocryphal New Testament* (London: Oxford University Press, 1966), vi-x. One of the best resources for study of this literature is *Lost Christianities* by Bart Ehrman of the University of North Carolina.

motives, such as peddling Gnostic teachings, pushing a particular brand of Christology, or seeking better Christian connections with Jewish or pagan roots.

No Priestly Conspiracy

Generally, the early church members could tell the difference between a spiritually solvent work like Ephesians (probably written by an admirer of Paul near the end of the first century) and works like the Infancy narratives (a grotesque pseudo-history in which a peeved young Jesus curses children, who subsequently die). There were, however, many samples of inspirational early writing (e.g., the Shepherd of Hermas and the Didache) which nevertheless did not find their way into the New Testament canon. With the rising popularity of non-canonical gospels—through the work of legitimate scholars like Elaine Pagels and Bart Ehrman, and with the commercial success of novels like *The DaVinci Code* with its highly speculative, intellectually oblivious romp through historical fiction—more people today than ever before are reading and becoming aware of these extra-biblical books.

Contrary to popular belief, there was no priestly conspiracy to keep these books away from the masses. During the formative years of the Christian faith, free market forces decided which books would constitute the Bible. All manuscripts were hand-copied, an expensive, labor-intensive project which only happened when a book was popular enough to justify the expenditure of resources.

Even so, authors continued to use names of Apostles and great figures from the first century to add validity to their ideas and authority to their works. In the fifth century a series of writings appeared which purported to flow from the pen of Dionysius, an early follower of the Apostle Paul, who received a one-line mention in the New Testament: "But some men joined him and believed, among them Dionysius the Areopagite."[7]

Lonely Eagle

These writings soon gained immense popularity and were widely held to be genuine works of the Apostolic age. Tillich discussed this mistake in his book, *A History of Christian Thought*:

---

7.   Acts 17:34, RSV.

Dionysius the Areopagite is the classic Christian mystic, one of the most interesting figures in Eastern church history. He was also of extreme importance in the West. In Acts 17:34 we read of a man called Dionysius who followed Paul after he had preached in the Areopagus (the famous Mars' Hill sermon). His name was used by a writer who lived around C.E. 500. In the tradition this man was accepted as the real Dionysius who talked with Paul.... It is an established historical fact that the man who wrote these books wrote around C.E. 500 and used the name of Paul's companion in Athens in order to lend authority to his books.[8]

Pseudo-Dionysius, whoever he was, brought a sunburst of light to the leading edge of the dark ages. All medieval and modern mysticism to come afterward has been directly or indirectly affected by this lone author. Laboring in secret at his desk, he wrestled with concepts like Divine Mind, the Silence, and the One Presence and One Power, which he had the foresight to glean from the pages of the Gospels. While the rest of Christianity amused itself by nit-picking about the Christological Controversies (on the nature and person of Jesus), Dionysius soared like a lonely eagle above these squabbles to reach for mystical union with God. His goal was Christ-consciousness, and his method was prayer and meditation on the unspeakable goodness of God. Dionysius wrote:

> Wherefore, it is above all necessary, especially in theology, to begin with prayer, not in order to attract to ourselves the power which is present everywhere and nowhere, but by commemorating and calling upon God to give ourselves into his hands and become one with him.[9]

Dionysius' attitude was wholly unlike that of his day. Where other early medieval churchmen heaped scorn and pronounced *anathemas* on their opponents, he urged Christians to refrain from attack thoughts and let Truth stand as its own defense. McGiffert observed:

---

8. Tillich, 90.
9. McGiffert, *Vol.* I, 293.

The contrast between his spirit and that of many other theologians of the age, is shown by his sixth letter addressed to the presbyter Sosipater, in which he exhorts him not to attack those that differ with him but to set forth the truth and let it speak for itself.[10]

In this way he anticipated the cooperative spirit of New Thought Christianity. Fillmore later echoed Dionysius' sentiments in *Talks on Truth:* "Love does not brag about its demonstrations. It simply lives the life, and lets its works speak for it."[11]

Oddly Familiar?

Metaphysical Christian affinities with these fifth century writings run far deeper. Except for his flowery style and complicated mythologies about angelic hierarchies, much of what Dionysius wrote could have come from the pen of New Thought authors. As each "new" idea finds its way into mystical Christianity of the modern age—whether by the fable of Richard Bach's *Jonathan Livingston Seagull,* the inspirational delights of poet James Dillet Freeman, or the speculations of modern mystic Neal Donald Walsh during his imaginative *Conversations with God*—it may be helpful to look backward along the course of church history to ask if these "new" thoughts are new after all.

Dionysius is a case in point. Writing at the trailing edge of the ancient era, fifteen hundred years ago, he taught some concepts which will sound oddly familiar to students of Metaphysical Christianity, to include: One Presence and One Power, God, the good omnipotent; nonexistence of evil as a power or force; the impersonal nature of God; the goal of all life is Christ-consciousness and union with the Divine; the importance of prayer; mysticism as the highest form of knowledge; the Silence (he called it *"the superessential brightness of the divine darkness...."*); use of symbolism in biblical interpretation; everything said about God is symbolic, since God is beyond comprehension and beyond human categories like good and perfection; God is also beyond the physical universe (hence, *meta*-physical); but God is present everywhere (hence, personal); all paths lead to God, but some lead more directly than others.

---

10. *Ibid.*
11. Charles Fillmore, *Talks on Truth* (Unity Village, MO: Unity Books, *1934),* 60.

A single volume on New Thought Christian history cannot hope to give adequate space to cover each "friend" in detail. However, even a brief look at an innovator like Dionysius would be incomplete without at least a fleeting glance at some of his more interesting doctrines. Four areas deserve special attention in Dionysius, i.e., his views on 1) God as One Presence/One Power, 2) nonexistence of evil, 3) the impersonal nature of God, and 4) symbolic theology.

Looking at the fresh-sounding words of Dionysius, it may become necessary to remember these ideas came from the mind of a Christian writer who lived a millennium and a half ago. And nowhere is the timeless quality of his thought more evident than in Dionysius' views on the absolute omnipotence and omnipresence of God.

1. One Presence/One Power.

Along with the divinity of each individual, the concept of God as One Presence and Power is perhaps the centermost teaching of Metaphysical Christianity. While Dionysius apparently did not explicitly mention the divinity of humanity, he certainly implied it:

> ...Hence all Being, all Power, all Activity, all Condition, all Perception, all Reason, all Intuition, all Apprehension, all understanding, all Communion—in a word, all that is-comes from the Beautiful and Good, hath its very existence in the Beautiful and Good, and turns toward the Beautiful and Good. Yea, all that exists and that comes into being, exists and comes into being because of the beautiful and Good; and unto this Object all things gaze and by It are moved and conserved, and for the sake of It, because of It and in It, existeth every originating Principle.[12]

Could there be a more cogent statement of the all-present, all-powerful nature of God? In hot pursuit of this high-flying concept, Dionysius quotes Romans 11:36 as evidence:

---

12. C. E. Rolt (trans.) *Dionysius the Areopagite* (NY: The Macmillan Co., *1951)*, 100.

For, as Holy Scripture saith: *'Of Him, and through Him, and to Him, are all things: to whom be glory for ever. Amen.'* And hence all things must desire and yearn for and must love the Beautiful and the Good.[13]

Although Paul's theology largely supports Dionysius' position, the above passage commits a major historical *faux pas*. The quote-within-a-quote exposes the thin disguise worn by a late fifth century impersonator. If this were a document from the hand of a New Testament era author, ostensibly at work during the lifetime of Paul, the original Dionysius would hardly have described a freshly penned *Letter to the Romans* as "Holy Scripture." Besides this, the pseudonymous writer would also have us believe that copies of Paul's private correspondence to the congregation at Rome were readily available to obscure citizens of Athens, where the Book of Acts places the "real" Dionysius.

Even medieval scholars caught this blunder, some of whom began to doubt the authenticity of Dionysius as a representative of the Apostolic age. Nevertheless, his inspirational forgeries continued to be copied and studied because of their mystical depth.

The Dionysian texts comprise ten brief letters and four major treatises, all encouraging the ruse of Apostolic authorship by bearing addresses to various persons in the first century church. The longest works, the four treatises, are directed to Timothy, supposedly the biblical character who traveled with Paul. The letters are addressed to other well-known first century personages, including the Apostle John.

Although he handled the reference material clumsily, Dionysius correctly saw an early Christian doxology in Paul's Letter to the Romans, a proto-doctrine which pointed beyond itself toward the concept of One Presence and One Power. The natural outgrowth of this insight for Dionysius was to see that if God is All-present and All-powerful, therefore anything which can be called *evil* can have no permanence. Dionysius even went beyond this idea to affirm, with modern Metaphysical Christians and neo-Platonists throughout history, that since evil is temporary, it has no real existence at all.

---

13. Ibid., 101.

2. Nonexistence of Evil.

If God is "the Beautiful and Good" from which everything "exists and comes into being," a logical conclusion can be drawn that evil cannot come from God. And since everything comes from God, evil cannot truly be said to exist. It is shadow, not substance. Dionysius writes:

> For even as fire cannot cool us, so Good cannot produce the things which are not good. And if all things that have been come from the Good...then nothing in the world cometh of evil. Then evil cannot even in any wise exist.[14]

One problem with this high-flying thought about the goodness of "all things" has always been the problem of evil. How can there be no evil when people encounter it in the world almost every day? Some evils are so monstrous that men of good will must fight back. Philosopher Jean-Paul Sartre was a pacifist as a young man, yet when the Nazi war machine invaded France and he experienced firsthand the horror of Hitler's scheme to create a master race, French intellectuals like Sartre took up arms and fought the evil which had befallen their country. Sartre was captured by the Germans in 1940 but escaped from prison camp the following spring. No longer a pacifist, he organized a French resistance group. Could a responsible person do otherwise, when confronted with the possibility of a world ruled by Adolf Hitler?

Dionysius was no dewy-eyed optimist. He knew people can choose to do terrible things to their fellow human beings, things rightly seen as evil. So, if everything comes from God, the beautiful and good, the question is how to reconcile this contradiction? His answer has become a common metaphor in New Thought: *Evil is the lack of good, just as dark is lack of light.* When someone puts out a lamp, darkness occurs. However, only light exists as a force, not darkness which is its absence. Dionysius would probably say that it makes no sense to sit in the dark while denying that darkness happens. However, there is no way to generate dark. Dark can only appear when light disappears, just as cold can only exist when heat is not present.

He never owned a refrigerator, but Dionysius would have immediately understood the principle of refrigeration is to remove heat. Air conditioners and deep freezers create no cold, they remove heat, resulting in a lesser heat,

---

14. Ibid., *111-112.*

expediently called *cold*. Although a fifth century thinker like Dionysius could not have known it, there is a point (minus 273 degrees centigrade) which marks the lowest possible temperature. Nothing can get colder than absolute zero, because at-273 C there is no heat whatsoever. So, the cold which people feel is really best understood as varying degrees of warmth. Heat alone has reality; cold is its absence.

As with light and heat, so goes good in opposition to evil. Evil has no power or reality; it is the absence of good. Dionysius believed that there are degrees in human character, too. Some souls are at a lower state of spirituality than others and so reflect less divine Light. Although one might reasonably call the actions of these persons *evil*, in reality they represent a lesser degree of good. Dionysius says:

> Some creatures participate wholly in the Good, others are lacking in
> It less or more, and others possess a still fainter participation therein,
> while to others the Good is present as but the faintest echo.[15]

This is due not to their nature but to their choices, Dionysius contended, since their natures are derived from God and are therefore Good. But what about the demons mentioned in Scripture? Surely they must be evil! Not so, wrote Dionysius. He boldly delivered this blow to demonology:

> Nor are the devils naturally evil. For, were they such, they would not
> have sprung from the Good...how can the devils be evil since they
> sprung from God? For the Good produceth and createth good
> things...they are not evil by their natural constitution but only
> through a lack of angelic virtues.[16]

Although Dionysius was a bold thinker, unafraid of controversy, one can understand his desire for medieval anonymity when reading passages like this.

3. Impersonal Nature of God—*Via Negativa.*

According to Dionysius, the supreme goal of life is to become one with God. This, he counseled, could be achieved only through mystical meditation and

---

15. Ibid., 114.
16. Ibid., 120-121.

prayer. However, he also believed in illumination as a tool to enhance mystical experiences. Dionysius, and through him many great thinkers afterward, taught that humans can best understand God by meditating on what He is not. Writing to "Timothy", pseudo-Dionysius encourages the younger man to seek the God beyond God:

> Do thou, dear Timothy, in thy eager striving…abandon both sense perception and mental activity…and as far as possible mount up with knowledge into union with the One who is above all being and knowledge; for by freeing thyself completely and unconditionally from thyself and from all things, thou shalt come to the superessential brightness of the divine darkness…[17]

His method of achieving spiritual illumination likewise employed an unconventional, mystical route, the *via negativa* or "way of negation." There are hints of Eastern theology in Dionysius, especially in his highly developed doctrine on the nature of God, approached by negation. Dionysius held that one only speaks meaningfully about God when articulating what the Divine is *not*: God is not limited, not restrained, not personal, etc. Yet, one can say accurately *God is good*, because Divine Mind is beyond goodness, or *God is love*, because the Lord is beyond loving-kindness. All statements about God must be affirmed and denied at the same time, because God is far beyond any meager effort at conceptualizing. Everything said about God is symbolic.

4. Symbolic Theology.

Dionysius provides a theological base for people like Paul Tillich, one of the twentieth century's most creative theologians, when the pseudo-Apostolic writer declares that all ideas of God are *symbolic*. God's transcendent nature demands that people must speak of the Divine in symbols. However, any image of God, dreamed up by limited human intelligence, must necessarily be wrong, because it will inevitably fall short of God's unknowable essence. Symbols are required, yet symbols are *a priori* false when used for God. Therefore, any symbol invented to talk about God must be affirmed and denied at the same time. Christian symbols—the Church as God's House, the Bible as God's Word, the Cross as God's presence and power even in the most excruci-

---

17. McGiffert, 304-306.

ating circumstances—can reveal the nature of God's healing love. But every symbol has the danger of becoming the reality it symbolizes. The Church becomes Christianity, instead of the gathered community seeking to become the beloved community, as it was in New Testament times; the Bible becomes the Word of God instead of the place where ancestors of the faith recorded their words about God; the Cross becomes the sign of bloody sacrifice and death instead of recalling the steadfast faith of Jesus in times of suffering and despair.

Dionysius influenced many thinkers who would come later. Thomas Aquinas, Meister Eckhart, and all the mystics after him would owe him a great debt. Sometimes, Dionysius begins to sound like he was read by some of the founding fathers-and-mothers of New Thought Christianity. Look at the amazing similarity between Dionysius and H. Emilie Cady:

> **Dionysius:** For as our sun, through no choice or deliberation, but by the very fact of its existence, gives light to all those things which have any inherent power of sharing its illumination, even so God sends forth upon all things according to their receptive powers, the rays of Its undivided Goodness.[18]

> **Cady:** We do not have to beseech God any more than we have to beseech the sun to shine. The sun shines because it is a law of its being to shine, and it cannot help it. No more can God help pouring into us unlimited wisdom, power, all good, because to give is a law of His being.[19]

One Presence/One Power, the nonexistence of evil as a force, the impersonal nature of God, symbolic theology. In these and other teachings the unknown author commonly called Dionysius anticipated the main thrust of New Thought theology more than fifteen hundred years ago.

Thankfully, Dionysius' work was not just allowed to collect dust on the shelves of monasteries. In the darkest hour of the Dark Ages another high-flying hero of the faith read the good news of God's One Presence and Power,

---

18. *Ibid.*
19. H. Emilie Cady, *Lessons in Truth* (Unity Village, MO: Unity Books), 34, 35.

then rose on wings of courage to reach an even higher understanding of the divine plan. This study now turns toward another lonely voice calling across the centuries from the Dark Ages of Church history, John Scotus Erigena.

5

Beyond the Night Sky

John Scotus Erigena
(Ninth Century C.E.)

Pseudo-Dionysius the Areopagite had penned his well-intended forgeries in *Koine*, a form of Greek derived from the classical language. Koine became the universal tongue of business and commerce in the late classical period, because Alexander the Great had left centers of Greek learning and culture in the wake of his world-wide conquests. Koine Greek became the *lingua franca* of Western civilization. Scholars are fairly unanimous that the New Testament was written neither in Hebrew (which by the time of Jesus was already a dead language), nor Aramaic (which the early followers and disciples probably spoke), but in Koine Greek, the language of international communication. Even Caesar's Roman officials spoke and wrote Greek; the official business of the Empire was often conducted in Koine.

With growing respectability and power, the Roman Church began to shift its internal correspondence to a simpler version of Latin, the Vulgate, or vernacular. St. Jerome translated the Bible into Latin Vulgate as early as the fifth century. However, Greek remained the language of Scripture and commerce in the Eastern half of the Roman Empire, and the split between Rome and Constantinople insured this breech would become permanent. Eastern orthodox churches today still read the Bible and conduct services mainly in Greek.

Since reading in any language was a highly specialized skill comparable to computer programmers today, few people outside the Church mastered the written word in their own language, let alone gained any facility in a foreign tongue. Because vernacular Latin was the common language of the Early

Medieval church in the West, it slowly but surely nudged Koine Greek out of the picture.

Ironically, once it had seized the center stage Latin refused to yield the limelight. As languages continued to evolve in Western civilization, Latin—like Hebrew, Aramaic, and classical Greek—became a dead language. However, Latin lingered for centuries as the official language of Church, scholarship and legal proceedings. Even today, some knowledge of Latin is a helpful tool for attorneys, and Latin has so powerfully gripped church theology and policy that official Catholic documents have continued to be composed in the language of the Caesars into the twenty-first century.

Jerome's Latin Vulgate Bible and the Latin Mass clung tenaciously to its position as the official tongue of the Roman Church long after the last Latin-speaking native linguist had died. This Latin-centrism was one of the reasons which prompted seventeenth century English political philosopher Thomas Hobbs to write in his *Leviathan*: "The Papacy is the ghost of the Roman Empire sitting crowned on the grave thereof."[1]

Even though Latin was introduced to bring the common language of the people into the church's worship and Scriptures, the Vulgate ironically became the greatest hindrance to popular understanding in the Western church. By the time of the next ancestor in the ancient faith, the ninth century, Latin was already a scholarly and priestly language quite distant from the illiterate masses, who could not even read their own languages. And this inability to read was not restricted to peasants. Kings, nobles, and virtually all women remained illiterate. Reading was a specialized skill, the exclusive province of the clergy. When the Bible was read, it was read by a clergyperson who gave the church's interpretation of what the text meant.

As Latin died out, the biblical witness became even further removed from the people—not only was it written, *it was written in a dead language*. The hold of the clergy on exclusive rights to interpret Truth was complete. Increasingly, people began to believe that God could be found only through the Church, which held the keys to both a heavenly kingdom reserved for the faithful and to earthy dungeons reserved for heretics.

The Irish Saved the World…Culturally

After the fall of Rome, world culture did an interesting flip-flop. Instead of the center of the former Empire, the very fringe of Roman civilization became

---

1.   Thomas Hobbes, *Leviathan*, Chapter XLVII.

the bank where learning was kept on deposit. Roman legions never conquered Scotland or Ireland, but Christian missionaries brought the fiercely independent Celts into the mainstream of civilization by converting them to the ancient faith. With typical zeal, the Irish embraced Christianity and set about establishing centers of study on the far northwest coast of their island nation.

In fact some historians, like Lord Kenneth Clark in his BBC series *Civilisation,* believe the Irish saved Western culture. It was these monasteries on the seaward, northwestern coast of Ireland and Scotland, the farthest edge of European civilization, which delivered Western culture from its dark night of the soul during the cultural anarchy following the fall of Rome, now known as the Dark Ages. Various writings from classical Greece and Rome survive only through copies laboriously penned by Irish monks sitting at their desks, fighting sleep and shivering from cold winds blowing off the North Atlantic. Historian Paul Johnson remarks that the scholars of the Dark Ages labored in the shadow of greater darkness to come:

> There was a sense of gloomy urgency about the task, for men believed that, however horrible the period since Rome's decline had been things would get worse, not better....[2]

In the ninth century, King Alfred insisted that his scholars press on with translation of the essential Latin texts into Old English because he firmly believed the time was fast approaching when no one would any longer be able to read Latin.[3] It was in this gathering intellectual long winter's night that one of the bright stars in the history of Christian thought rose over the Irish horizon.

His name was John, but in the medieval period middle names and surnames were not usually handed down within families. Celebrated personages often became known by accomplishments or attributes, and not always auspicious ones at that. *William the Conqueror* was a mighty moniker, but what king would enjoy being remembered by posterity as *Ethelred the Unready?* Certainly, the lionized name of *Charles the Great* (Charlemagne) was more than adequate, but what about poor *Charles the Bald,* shorn forever like a bad hair day in history? By far the most common last names given by history to great figures of the past are related to geography: *Francis of Assisi, Joan of Arc, Cathe-*

---

2. Johnson, *157.*
3. Ibid.

rine of Siena, and so on. Since John came from Ireland *(Scotus* in Latin), he became known as John the Irishman born in Erin or *Johannes Scotus Erigena.*

Sharp Mind, Quick Wit

In his multi-volume work of an earlier generation, *The Story of Civilization*, Will Durant says that Erigena was neither a clergyman nor a monk, yet he was a man of vast learning, quite competent in Greek and knowledgeable in the classics. He also reports that John was "something of a wit," as the following anecdote at the royal banquet table indicates:

> Charles the Bald, dining with him asked him, *"What distinguishes* (literally, *'what separates')* a fool from an Irishman?"* to which John is said to have answered, *"The table."*[4]

Erigena must have been educated in Irish schools related to the monasteries in some way, for he displays an extraordinary knowledge of theology and church doctrine as well as Greek. He was born around the year 810 and moved to France in the 840's where he became the in-house scholar and theologian for King Charles. Despite Erigena's counter-barb, or perhaps because of it, Charles the Bald decided he liked John and protected him when the theologian ran into trouble with church authorities over doctrinal arguments.

This relationship between a secular ruler and a radical religious thinker anticipates a similar bond which will exist in the sixteenth century between Frederick the Wise and the radical-thinking Martin Luther. Both John in the ninth century and Luther in the sixteenth had the good fortune and common sense to win support from people who held the reins of power in their immediate vicinity. Without this relationship, both would have been just two more heretics burned at the stake.

This suggests that, despite the idealism which characterizes John's writings, he knew the cynical secular world has its own golden rule: the people with the gold make the rules. Less realistic reformers have not lasted long enough to make such an impact as Luther or Erigena.

---

4. Will Durant, *The Story* of *Civilization, Vol. IV, The Age* of *Faith* (NY: Simon & Schuster, *1950), 477.* Parenthesis in the original.

Controversy Begins

John got into trouble the first time during a debate over the sacraments, but his writings on this subject have not survived. What has been preserved are the cries of Erigena's opponents that John did not believe in the "real presence" of Jesus Christ's body and blood in the eucharistic meal. They reported that Erigena considered them a symbolic rather than literal presence. More than this is not known.

However, in the next controversy John gathered enough notoriety to be fully documented. The German monk Gottschalk was preaching absolute predestination, denying that men and women have free will. Predestination has been debated in the Christian church since the early days. Augustine held this view, and later the great Protestant reformer John Calvin, made Calvinism almost synonymous with predestination. Most Christian thought has usually leaned toward human freedom and away from the fatalism of predestination, but the Middle Ages saw a high degree of interest in the intractable, eternal consistency of God's mighty plan. Perhaps more people held fatalistic views in medieval times than in any other time before or since; in times of short life expectancy and little comfort, an obdurate God with an established agenda seemed like a good bargain.

Archbishop Hincmar saw Gottschalk's preaching as dangerous. As Pelagius had pointed out in his debate with Augustine, if humans do not believe they have free will, the Church has relieved them of the responsibility to make ethical and moral decisions. A believer in absolute predestination can comfortably ignore poverty, war, racism, and nuclear proliferation. If all of this was determined long ago and no one has any free moral agency, all human effort is equally pointless. Thus in a very paradoxical way those who believe in total predestination are actually in league with those who believe in no God at all, for both see human values operating fruitlessly. The atheist says there are no eternal, moral standards because no God exists; the predestinarian says it's irrelevant because humans have no power to act, morally or otherwise, so God's will alone determines what is good or evil.[5]

---

5. To be fair to my predestinarian friends, Protestant moralists have never advocated anything like anti-nomianism or a hippie-like moral leeway due to the predestined nature of Reality. Right the contrary, the moral impetus which has dominated Protestantism has often come from a strong desire to show that the individual believer is one of the Elect. One could assume a soul predestined to heaven would know how to behave itself on earth, and a life which shows otherwise would not be a good indicator for eternity.

Erigena's reputation as a scholar and controversialist earned him an invitation from Hincmar to write a refutation of Gottschalk. John accepted, gleefully cutting a swath through not only Gottschalk's predestination, but the whole concept of any restraint on the exercise of human freedom and reason. He charged Gottschalk with heresy and ignorance, because God not only allows people the right to choose evil but He really doesn't know what they are going to choose, either. If God knew evil, He would be the cause of it, Erigena declared.

Questioning Authority

More profound, however, was his attack on the principles of church authority and tradition. John was a Christian philosopher in an age when philosophy was highly suspect. In the medieval period one did not speculate or use new arguments to discover Truth. The pattern was to find an ancient authority and quote it, preferably, an ancient orthodox church father. Scientific investigation and experimentation, such as taken for granted today, was simply not part of the mental equipment. Hundreds of years after Erigena, the Church would call before its Inquisition an aging Galileo and force him to recant his heretical notion that the Earth revolves around the sun. Although Galileo had looked through his telescope and seen the universe firsthand, such evidence was not admissible because it conflicted with the ancient authorities.

Yet, even if ancient authorities were the singular basis for determining truth during medieval times, Erigena would have none of this. He launched his attack on Gottschalk by praising the methods of philosophical speculation:

> In earnestly investigating and attempting to discover the reason of
> all things, every means of attaining to a pious and perfect doctrine
> lies in that science and discipline which the Greeks call philosophy.[6]

Erigena's refutation was more heretical than Gottschalk's sermons. Councils in 855 and 859 condemned both of them. Gottschalk remained a prisoner at his monastery until his death; but John's patron, Charles, protected the Quixotic, uncompromising Irishman.

Other currents of history were moving to bring into John's hands the work of another friend, Dionysius the Areopagite, met in the previous study. As

---

6.   Ibid.

mentioned earlier, by this time Christendom had split into two major subdivisions, East and West. The Eastern Church was known as the Byzantine Empire because its capital at Constantinople was built on the site of a town previously known as Byzantium. Of course, the Eastern Church still spoke Greek, since its greatest population was ethnically Greek.

Dionysius Re-mix

In 824 the Byzantine Emperor Michael the Stammerer sent a copy of Dionysius' works to the Western Church. However, since it was in Koine Greek, no one could read it, even at the highest levels of church and state. No one, that is, but a great scholar educated in Ireland, John Scotus Erigena. Although they doubted his orthodoxy, they never questioned his ability. He got the manuscript and proceeded to translate the wildly mystical writings of Pseudo-Dionysius into medieval Latin. Of course, at this time everyone still believed the works were genuine products of the Apostolic age, so the Dionysian texts carried special status in a world dominated by appeals to ancient authority.

John fell in love with the Dionysian writings, culling from their pages ideas like the nonexistence of evil, allegorical interpretation of the Bible, and other neo-Platonic concepts which the Eastern Church with its penchant for mystical theology had long favored. The West, following the lead of Tertullian and Augustine, became legalistic. Salvation was put in terms of obedience to Church and God, in that order. In the Eastern Church, the longstanding tradition had been to see Christianity as a mystical religion through which believers became united with God in Christ.

Sitting alone in his study, John Scotus Erigena discovered this difference in the writings of Dionysius. From that time forward, John was freed from legalism and ready to explore intellectually the idea that there is only One Presence and Power, God the Good, Omnipotent. He abandoned whatever shreds of legalism his mind had clung to and took off on a speculative flight unprecedented in the history of world religious thinking. McGiffert summarizes Erigena's vision:

> The divine nature embraces everything; apart from God or outside
> of him there is nothing. He is Being unlimited and undifferentiated;
> the world is Being circumscribed and divided. The unity between
> God and the creature is complete, he is in all things and is the being
> of all. When we say that God created everything, we mean that he is

in everything as its essence, the common substance of all that is Spirits and bodies, all things that exist are but manifestations of him; each is a genuine theophany.[7]

Above the Flock in a Dark Sky

God is not only omnipresent. For Erigena, God and man are in unity, bound so tightly they really are not two but one. John appealed to the Bible but was in no way hampered by it. He assumed difficulties with Scripture were to be read as allegory. Erigena writes:

> Do not be alarmed, for now we must follow reason which investigates the truth of things, and overpowered by no authority and in no way shackled, sets forth and proclaims openly what it has studiously examined and laboriously discovered.[8]

If medals were awarded for heroism retroactive to the ninth century, John the Irishman should receive the Medal of Honor. The courage it took to stand alone at the height of the Dark Ages and proclaim Truth as he saw it, regardless of the response of authority, can scarcely be grasped by people who live in a free society. People were broken on the rack for much less. Yet, John continued to teach Truth fearlessly, though council after council, Pope after Pope, ruled his works heretical. He responded to the anathemas from churchly authority with characteristic coolness:

> Authority sometimes proceeds from reason, but reason never from authority. For all authority that is not approved by true reason seems weak. But true reason, since it rests on its own strength, needs no reinforcement.[9]

Will Durant poetically observed, "Here is the Age of Reason moving in the womb of the Age of Faith."[10] It would take centuries before Christianity became practical again, drawing its beliefs from the core of biblical teachings

---

7. McGiffert, *173*.
8. Ibid.
9. Ibid., 170.
10. Durant, *477*.

and demonstrating them in everyday life. Appeal to authority would continue unabated until the revolutionary thinking of people like George Fox, William Ellery Channing, Ralph Waldo Emerson, and Theodore Parker, whose contributions to Christian thought will be explored in subsequent studies.

Unfettered by the limitations of official doctrine, Erigena's mind sailed like Jonathan Livingston Seagull, above the flock. Unafraid, he soared beyond the night sky of the Dark Ages to greet the eternal sunrise of Divine Truth. This brief study cannot leave his thought without examining Erigena's central thesis, an idea which would wait eleven centuries until another great thinker, Pierre Teilhard de Chardin, took it up again. As early as the mid-ninth century, John Scotus Erigena was talking about cosmic evolution/involution.

Four Stages of Divine Evolution/Involution

1) **God as Uncreated, Eternal.** This is where John begins his system. Just as astrophysics tells us that over fifteen billion years ago there was an aggregation of all matter in a great mass which exploded outward (the Big Bang theory), theological writers like Erigena, and much later Teilhard, see all existence issuing from God. In essence, John believed God created everything out of Himself. Applying Erigena's concepts to a scientific cosmology, one could say God has flung bits of Divinity to the far corners of the Cosmos, where they are destined to grow to awareness of their oneness with God. For Erigena, this happens in stages. Stage one begins with God, Who sends forth divine ideas, which are stage two.

2) **Divine ideas.** These are the models from which everything is created. God's creative power moves from pure energy to organization of reality. A modern analogy might see this as God's game plan for all time. Everything which exists flows from these divine ideas. In this John Scotus echoes John's gospel, which proclaims the Logos (Divine Mind) through Whom everything was created.

3) **World of Sensation.** All created things are part of the sensible world, the physical world. Matter is not eternal for Erigena, but came into being as the divine ideas worked their game plan. Matter is real, but not everlasting. All things and all beings are really God-power manifested in different form. As time passes, all will be taken back up into God.

4) Consummation. Teilhard calls this the *Omega Point*; New Thought Christians might call it Christ-consciousness. God sends forth energy to create divine ideas, and through these creates all things while giving all sentient beings free will to find the way back to God once more. For John Scotus Erigena, Jesus Christ is absolutely essential to this process, because in Jesus people have an open door to their own Christ-consciousness. Through faith in Jesus, humans are quite literally new creations.

Not all New Thought Christians will agree with everything he taught, but they can certainly marvel that such ideas were possible a thousand years before Darwin explained the process of evolution and progressive Christian thinkers pointed to a parallel in human spiritual development. Yet, this is precisely the point of all these investigations—New Thought is not new. Glimmers of these ideas have reappeared again and again in the history of Christianity. Often opposed by orthodox authority, such imaginative interpretations of the Christian witness have surfaced other places in the thinking and prayer life of these underground saints.

It is not mere speculation which makes John Scotus Erigena one of the fathers of Metaphysical Christianity; speculation can be a lazy man's excuse to avoid theological homework. Rather, it is because Erigena stood within the Church and doggedly refused to let orthodoxy define the terms for him. For this he deserves applause and thanks.

> True authority does not oppose right reason, nor right reason true authority. For it is not to be doubted that both come from one source, namely, the divine wisdom.[11]

John Scotus Erigena was a Christian philosopher, speculative genius, and a heroic yet unorthodox churchman. He qualifies as another spiritual ancestor of New Thought, an innovative pioneer who nudged humanity along its path toward better understanding of the Divine. His profound insights are still worthy of consideration today, twelve hundred years after he lived.

Now the study shifts to the last medieval churchman to be explored. The high mysticism of the Middle Ages found no greater expression than in the sermons and writings of a Dominican priest who joyfully proclaimed the divinity of humanity to his bewildered congregation. He was such as important figure that no text could be written about medieval theology which failed

---

11. Ibid.

to mention this unorthodox preacher. His beliefs almost cost him his life, but his tenacity in the face of danger has immeasurably enhanced the body of Christian mystical writings. The journey through mystical Church history leads next to Meister Eckhart.

6

Spark of the Soul

Meister Eckhart
(1260–1327 C.E.)

Something powerful and deep percolates in the works of the Dominican friar named Eckhart, whom history has dubbed *Meister* (master). Meister Eckhart had a world-embracing vision and a zeal for God. He was a God-intoxicated soul, like the great Hasidic Rabbis, or Catholic mystics like Catherine of Siena, or Protestant lovers of God like the Wesleys, who founded Methodism.

The Meister wrote intellectually, but sometimes divine love overflowed and he threw aside logic to proclaim his joy in the Lord, as when he shouted, "Up, noble Soul, put on thy dancing shoes!"

Eckhart wrote in Latin and German, but neither language could adequately express the vastness of his view of the divine panorama. Here are a few brief examples:

> God is infinite in his simplicity and simple in his infinity. Therefore he is everywhere and is everywhere complete. God is in the innermost part of each and every thing...When I think about the kingdom of God, I am struck dumb by its grandeur; for the kingdom of God is God Himself with all his fullness...all the worlds one could imagine God creating would still not be as the kingdom of God.... Nobody ever wanted anything as much as God wants to bring people to know him. God is always ready but we are not ready. God is

near to us but we are far from him. God is within; we are without. God is at home; we are abroad.[1]

And this passage about God's love:

> Now, you must know that God loves the soul so strenuously that to take this privilege of loving from God would be to take his life and being. It would be to kill God, if one may use such an expression. For out of God's love for the soul, the Holy Spirit blooms and the Holy Spirit is that love. Since, then, the soul is so strenuously loved by God, it must be of great importance....[2]

Eckhart's writing echoes in the words of Charles Fillmore and Ernest Holmes. Like modern New Thought teachers, he was not afraid to follow a line of thought wherever it took him, because he was rooted firmly in divine truth and held love for God above all else. More importantly for students of Metaphysical Christianity, Eckhart's mysticism sprang from the belief that saw the Good as omnipotent, all-pervasive. And he was not hesitant to dip into non-Christian sources to find others who shared his viewpoints. He quotes the celebrated medieval rabbi Moses Maimonides, who has been called the greatest Jewish scholar of all time. Even more daringly, during a time of hostility between Moslems and Christians, Eckhart showed his universalism by reading, studying and quoting the brilliant medieval Islamic philosophers Averroes and Avicenna. It never occurred to Eckhart that he should observe any racial, religious, or ethnic barriers in pursuit of Truth. God was his objective; he would not be slowed by anything or anyone in his dance of Divine love.

From Peasant to Chair

Little is known of Eckhart's early life. He was born Johannes Eckhart, probably in the year 1260. In those days births were seldom recorded unless the child was heir to a title or property holdings, and little John Eckhart had nei-

---

1.   Walter Holden Capps and Wendy M. Wright, (eds.), *Silent Fire* (San Francisco: Harper Forum Books, *1978*), 112, 114.
2.   Ibid., 115.

ther. However, he did have a keen intellect and was soon enrolled as a novice of the Dominican Friars at Erfurt, Germany.

For centuries, children of low birth had few avenues for upward mobility. Bound to the land as serfs under the feudal system, the common people were essentially slaves to the noble lord who presided over the town or country estate or *manor*. They were not permitted an education, nor were they allowed to join the military service except as pack carriers and work crews. These careers offered no more benefits than landed serfdom, so most peasants dreaded the frequent wars that swept through their lands taking human lives and subsistence crops from poor villages.

Yet, one avenue offered escape for children of exceptional promise. In the Middle Ages the Church guarded the gateway to education and advancement, the sole place where a young person of ability and ambition could rise on merit to a position of some respectability and power. It cost the youth his right to marry and have relationships with members of the opposite sex, not to mention the grueling pace of monastic life, but in a world of serfdom this was a price worth paying.

Johannes Eckhart chose this course. A bright lad, he joined the Dominican order, where he would be able to develop his preaching skills and have a good chance for further education, perhaps even university professorships. Various religious orders took on special functions as the structure of medieval Christianity evolved. The Dominicans became known as the Preaching Order because public speaking was their specialty.

Arabs had founded the university system centuries before Eckhart's time. As this departmentalized form of education spread to the West, colleges established teaching posts, which to this day are called *chairs*. Not to be confused with today's politically correct abbreviation for *chairperson*, the academic *chair* refers to an established, tenured lecture appointment. There was a chair of history, chair of theology, chair of biblical studies, and so on. These chairs were the exclusive property of religious orders, so the Dominicans jealously guarded their teaching posts and ensured that their people filled the Dominican chairs. Orders which did not have access to these positions were always vying to get a man into a chair so they could set a precedent for the future. So, orders with teaching chairs were careful whom they sent to the post, since they prized these jobs so highly.

The Dominicans chose Johannes Eckhart to continue his studies at the University of Paris and groomed him for higher placement. He was eventually given lectureships and finally a chair. This means young Eckhart was an outstanding churchman, far above his peers. No one of less ability would obtain such a post, lest he fail at the job and be replaced by someone of another order. Eckhart lectured competently at the University of Paris, held various important administrative positions in his order, and generally displayed good rapport within his brotherhood and the Church at large.

In fact, he might never have caused controversy had it not been for another aspect of his role as a Dominican, that of itinerant preacher. Meister Eckhart made no attempt to conceal his mysticism as he preached from pulpit after pulpit in the German vernacular, the common language of the people. Often his congregations were comprised of nuns under his spiritual guidance. His sermons must have flown high over the heads of ordinary folks, but his popularity was enormous.

Thomism: The Aquinas Connection

To understand Meister Eckhart one must understand Scholasticism, the new philosophy of the high Middle Ages championed by his predecessor in Paris, Thomas Aquinas. It would be Eckhart's contribution to Christianity to take the intellectual concepts of Scholasticism and give them expression through prayer, mystical practices, and preaching. Paul Tillich describes his role:

> They (the medieval mystics) were not speculative monks sitting alongside of the world, but they wanted people to have the possibility of experiencing what was expressed in the scholastic systems. Thus the mysticism of Eckhart unites the most abstract scholastic concepts—especially that of being—with a burning soul, with the warmth of religious feeling and the love-power of religious acting.[3]

Since Meister Eckhart was a Dominican and a mystic, it was natural that he should employ mysticism in service of the great concepts annunciated by the paramount religious scholar of medieval times, Thomas Aquinas. Where Thomas had been a thinker, Eckhart was a preacher and a doer. The Meister wanted humans to experience God, not just read about Him. The influence of *Thomism* prevails to this day, but when Eckhart began his ministry, Aquinas had just died. In fact, the two men were contemporaries and might have known each other if Thomas had not died in 1275 at age fifty. It remained for

---

3.   Tillich, 201.

the greatest Dominican mystic, Meister Eckhart, to make practical and apply the ideas of the greatest Dominican scholar, the "angelic Doctor" St. Thomas Aquinas. To understand either man's contribution to New Thought Christianity requires a comprehension of both.

Back to Athens: Two Rivals

To comprehend the Scholasticism of medieval times, one must return to ancient Greece and examine the contrasting philosophies of two other contemporaries, Plato and Aristotle. As students of world history know, Socrates taught Plato; Plato taught Aristotle; and Aristotle taught Alexander the Great, who tried to teach the world. Greek culture spread widely and the Greek language became the *lingua franca* of the educated ancient world because of Alexander's efforts at intellectual and cultural missionary work, to the point that some historians feel Alexander is the most influential figure in Western history—surpassing even Jesus and Paul—because of his establishment of a cultural and linguistic framework on which Indo-European society was built.

Of course, Alexander wanted to spread, not the ideas of Socrates and Plato, but the theories of his own master, Aristotle. One would think that with all this chain of command in educational matters, the philosophies of Plato and Aristotle would be highly compatible. Yet, Aristotle repudiated the central thesis of his teacher's worldview and postulated a radically different view of reality than Platonist idealism. Plato had held that true reality is in an unseen ideal world, the world of divine ideas. He taught that human beings were capable of directly contacting this unseen realm and gaining personal insights into ultimate reality. In fact, a true Platonist might even doubt that matter has any reality. Only in the realm of divine ideas do seekers find real Truth.

Aristotle, on the other hand, insisted human knowledge comes precisely through experiences in and of the world, not by abstract discussion as Plato favored. For Aristotelians, observation, not speculation, is king of thought. Of course, for a religion built on authority, biblical texts, and Church tradition, Aristotle's call for people to look at the world with fresh eyes was a dangerous heresy. The Church had decreed *Plato, yes; Aristotle, no.*[4] McGiffert wrote:

> Nothing could well be more opposed than these two views. They represent indeed two radically different philosophical tendencies. It

---

4. McGiffert, *Vol.* II, 260.

is evident at a glance that such a theory of knowledge such as Aristotle's was out of line with traditional Christian ideas.[5]

Aristotle: The Medieval Darwinism

Churchmen violently opposed Aristotelianism when it began seeping into Christendom through Muslim Spain. Like the Irish monks during the Dark Ages, enlightened Arab scholars saved another large chunk of ancient philosophy and literature for modern humanity to wrestle with and enjoy. In its early years, Islam had no problem with innovative ideas from the West.

However, this new burst of Aristotelianism caused quite a flurry in medieval Europe. This initial resistance to Aristotle had its parallel in the great outcry of conservative churchmen over the theories of Charles Darwin at the end of the nineteenth century. Most intelligent Christians quickly realized evolution was an idea whose time had come and could not be ignored without *Spark of the Soul* great peril to the cause of Truth. Even though the opponents of evolution tend to be a vocal minority clamoring to be heard, the great majority of Christian scholars today accept the scientific fact of evolution and no longer see it as opposed to biblical legends, myths and stories. Evolution cannot be denied without objecting to the way God has primarily orchestrated life in the Cosmos. If God has created a system by which non-life evolves to life and on to intelligence, who are mortals to dispute with Divine Order? Various Christians theologies are optional; the fact of evolution is here to stay.

Likewise, Thomas Aquinas and those who came after him in the scholastic tradition realized that Aristotle was a force to be reckoned with, not shouted down nor ignored. Thomas set to work reinterpreting traditional doctrines by the light Aristotelian logic. McGiffert again:

> In spite of the difficulties Thomas combined Aristotelianism and Christian theology and he did it by drawing two sharp distinctions: the one between natural and revealed theology and the other between the condition of knowledge in this life and in the next.[6]

---

5. *Ibid.*
6. Ibid. For a more comprehensive treatment of Aquinas's struggles with the Platonic-Aristotelian synthesis, see the chapter on Thomas Aquinas in A *History* of Christian Thought, Vol. 2, by McGiffert.

Spark of the Soul

At the risk of gross oversimplification—an offense which a survey like this must risk in order to cover so much territory so quickly—here is how Aquinas seems to have resolved the conflict. Thomas held both Plato and Aristotle were right; there is an unseen realm which contains divine ideas, yet humans know things of this world only through the senses. The belief that God can be discovered through the power of reason was from Aristotle. This is a kind of reaching upward toward heaven. But humans learn about God more perfectly through His revelation to humanity, especially His revelation in Jesus Christ. This is modified Platonism. It combines natural theology (Aristotelian reaching upward) and revealed religion (Platonic divine ideas known directly in Jesus Christ).[7]

Meister Eckhart took this raw scholastic data and produced a remarkable life of faith based on its central teachings. But where Thomas insisted that full knowledge of God is possible in the Platonic sense only in the world to come, Eckhart claimed people can have it here. Not full knowledge of God in His completeness, but a glimmer of that completeness. He called the place where God is known to an individual person the *Seelenfuenklein* or *"spark of the soul."* It was a highly controversial theology in his day and provoked predictable outrage from Church leaders.

Eckhart believed humans can know God three ways: *sensibly, rationally,* and *super-rationally.* Through the senses, a seeker can detect the hallmark of God's presence in the world. The rational mind logically infers a Source of goodness and beauty. However, only when abandoning sensory pursuits and rational inquiry, only when mounting up on wings of praise and ecstasy, will the soul rise to an unshakeable awareness of God's reality. If someone communes with God, loves and lives for Him, questions about Divine existence seem superfluous and absurd. This is the essence of what Eckhart said, and he went beyond this basic awareness to speak in even more intimate terms about relationship to the Divine.

Oneness with God

Humans can know God because they are one with God. This union is not just a harmony of wills or a spiritual communion; Eckhart envisions complete

---

7. Capps & Wright, 111.

fusion of the individual with God like a drop of water returning to the sea. He took the biblical concept of *imago Dei* literally; humans were in fact created in the image of God. In a sermon on "Renewal in the Spirit," he told his congregation:

> God must become I, and I must become God....The fire changes into itself whatever is brought to it, and gives it its own nature. The wood does not change the fire into wood, rather the fire changes wood into fire. Thus we are transformed into God and know him as he is.[8]

Eckhart assumed God and humanity could be united because they were already one. Not simply made in the image and likeness of God, they share in the very nature of God. The *imago Dei* means humans are truly divine beings, offspring of God the Father. The key is consciousness.

> If the wood knew about God and were conscious how near he is, as the highest angel is conscious of it, the wood would have the same blessedness as the angel.[9]

What about human consciousness? Eckhart assured his flock that they participated in greater blessings because they had greater awareness of their divine nature.

> Therefore man is more blessed than a stick of wood, because he recognizes God and knows how near God is. The more conscious of it the more blessed, the less conscious of it the less blessed he is. He is not blessed because God is in him and near to him, or because he has God, but only because he is aware of God.[10]

All God Concepts Fall Short

Eckhart and other mystics in Christian tradition believed direct communion between the individual worshiper and God was possible. What separated him

---

8. McGiffert, 360-361.
9. *Ibid.*, 365.
10. Ibid., 362-363.

from other mystics was this proclamation of the oneness of God and man. He has often been accused of *pantheism*, the belief that everything is God—the tree, the stone, men and women. Pantheism reduces God to the sum total of all things; God is the universe. Eckhart would not agree, because his concept of God far transcended the mere physical universe.

The best modern term for Eckhart's doctrine of God is probably *panentheism*.[11] The idea has become increasingly more popular in New Thought and mainstream Christian thought and shows real potential for uniting a series of apparently disjunctive concepts about the relationship of humanity to the Divine Power and to the Cosmos.

Panentheism, simply described, says that everything and everyone is in God as a fish is in water. This advanced concept echoes ancient ideas, as the well-known New Testament quote, attributed by Luke to Paul's sermon on Mars Hill in Athens and found at Acts 17:28, "For 'In him we live and move and have our being'; as even some of your own poets have said." Depending on which scholarly source is consulted, the *poet* credited by Acts could be either Epimenides or Posidonius, both Greek philosophers.

One might even imagine a *monistic panentheism*, which extends beyond *pantheism* to include not only the transcendent and immanent but all the principles and laws of existence, as well as physical matter, energy, and any spiritual realms which may exist. More than fish and ocean, this God-concept embraces the all the principles of chemistry and physics by which the ocean exists and operates. Applying the term to Fillmorean theology: *God is mind, idea, expression.* It is a concept which New Thought writers are just beginning to explore, yet the roots of panentheism go deep.[12]

Panentheism has strong defenders in post-Modern Christian thought, to include Matthew Fox, one of the world's foremost Eckhartian scholars:

> For Eckhart it is basically wrong to think of God as a Person "out there" or even of God as wholly Other "out there." God is in us and we are in God. This is the theology of inness and of panentheism which form the basis of Eckhart's God talk and consciousness.[13]

---

11. See my "Evolution of the God Concept" found at Appendix C.
12. Ibid.
13. Matthew Fox, *Passion for Creation: The Earth-Honoring Spirituality of Meister Eckhart* (Rochester, VT: Inner Traditions, 2000), 44.

In fact, the Meister had a concept of divinity so lofty he acknowledged the futility of all concepts to express the inexpressible depth of God. "If you can understand anything about him," he writes, "it in no way belongs to him."[14] Any comprehensible God-concept must necessarily be wrong, falling far short of the true grandeur of divinity, which God alone perceives about Himself. Eckhart did not advise against theology, but felt intellectual critique and reconstruction must be buttressed by personal experience with the Divine. The Meister wanted a God-experience, not just a theoretical model.

In places Eckhart's writings are sheer poetry. He coaxes his parishioners to turn wholly to God and enter the silence of His presence through prayer and meditation. He even taught centering prayer—using that term—like the guided meditations widely practiced in Metaphysical Christianity today. And how does a soul ascend unto divinity? Eckhart thought the essence of spiritual growth could be summed up in one word: *detachment*. He writes: "True detachment means a mind as little moved by what befalls, by joy and sorrow, honor and disgrace, as a broad mountain by a gentle breeze."[15]

Why detachment? Because God is free from all worries and problems; God is the Infinite and lacks nothing. Since He lacks nothing, He needs nothing. He is motionless, still, silent, beyond thought and action, beyond all possible concepts. God appears to us only in the *Seelenfuenklein*, the spark of the soul where God touches finite minds with a hint of divinity, and then only as a feeling which sounds absurd when describing the experience to others. The Meister was saying in Medieval language what James Dillet Freeman will write in his poem *"I Am There"*, and Astronaut James Irwin will leave on the moon for space travelers to come:

> Only in absolute stillness, beyond self, can you know Me as I AM, and then but as a feeling and a faith.[16]

In all this other voices continually echo: Philo, Origen, Dionysius, and Erigena, as well as hints of those yet to be discussed: Fox, Emerson, Tillich, and

---

14. Edmund Colledge and Bernard McGinn (trans.), *Meister Eckhart, Classics of Western Spirituality* (NY: Paulist Press, 1981), 207.
15. McGiffert, 371.
16. James Dillet Freeman, "I Am There," free verse prayer-poem, published in pamphlets and posters by Unity School of Christianity; available online at multiple sites.

Chardin. McGiffert says that Eckhart reminds him of Dionysius, and especially of Erigena. McGiffert says:

> Whether Eckhart drew directly upon that great thinker (Erigena)…at any rate his (Eckhart's) thought moved along similar lines. Not altogether inappropriately he might be called a mystical Erigena or Erigena become mystic.[17]

Controversy Poorly Handled

Eckhart was attacked by more conservative churchmen, as prophets tend to be. His works were condemned in a Papal bull (decree) *"In Agro Dominico"* which translates from the Latin *"In the Field of the Lord,"* the phrase with which the bull begins. Note the Latin wording is perhaps a play on the word *Dominican,* reflecting power politics between Eckhart's Dominican order and other groups within the Church. The bull was published after a series of charges had been leveled against him by church officials. Eckhart handled the attack un-masterfully. Startled by controversy over what he thought were obvious points in doctrine and faith, Eckhart replied to the charges by denying any of them were true and heaping abuse upon those who doubted his orthodoxy. His tactic was not effective; the charges stood. Eckhart died before the bull was made public, cheating the hangman, so to speak, and avoiding any possible punishment for his alleged heresy.

His legacy to modern mystical Christianity remains profound. He saw the world, like Erigena before him, as part of an eternal process of evolution/involution, unfolding and refolding, growth and change. He believed the scholastics were right, that there is evidence for God in the physical world and in the realm of ideas. He took these abstract concepts and put them into practice. In this respect, he might be called the first father of practical Christianity.

The Father and All Are One

Always reaching for the unattainable, Eckhart had the courage to say from the pulpit that God and man are a unity. He told the German nuns—no doubt to their astonishment if they followed his argument at all—that he and the Father were One:

---

17. McGiffert, 365.

The eye wherewith I see God is, the same eye wherewith God sees me. My eye and God's eye are one eye—one seeing, one knowing, one loving...I say more: he begets me not alone as his Son, he begets me as himself and himself as me—me his essence and his nature.[18]

With the ecstatic words of Meister Eckhart ringing through the ages, this study leaves those marvelous medieval mystics and move to the next major group of forerunners to Metaphysical Christianity. In the works of George Fox, Georg Hegel, Ralph Waldo Emerson, and his disciple Theodore Parker, reside all the spiritual, intellectual, and systematic foundations on which nineteenth century metaphysicians will construct the movement known as New Thought. So this period—from the late days of the radical reformation of the seventeenth century through the Enlightenment to the Unitarian Controversy of the nineteenth century—is called *"Setting the Stage."* It will prove an apt description.

---

18. Ibid., 362-363.

III

Setting the Stage

7

The Cheerful Walker

George Fox
(1624–1691 C.E.)

How does one describe a man like George Fox? In any age he would be extraordinary. Unlettered, he challenged and triumphed over learned adversaries. Untitled, he took on the power of the established Church of England which was backed by the King. Uncultured, he attracted followers from the humblest to the highest levels of society. Unordained, he founded a religious movement which spanned two continents and has wielded tremendous influence on Western civilization. Unafraid, he stood before judges and rulers who had the power to imprison, physically chastise, and even kill him for his religious views.

Through it all, he managed to maintain a positive, healthy attitude and a firm belief that Truth would prevail. He told the ministers and missionaries who went forth teaching his vision of a Christianity restored that they were to "walk cheerfully over the earth, answering that of God in everyone."[1] In the symbolic language he used, this meant go forth with faithful confidence, drawing out of everyone you meet their own indwelling Christ light. His contribution to modern Metaphysical Christianity was to be the first to teach the Inner Light, which is Christ within.

---

1. Howard H. Brinton, *The Religion of George Fox* (Lebanon, PA: Pendle Hill, 1968), 11.

Dangerous Times

George Fox lived in dangerous times. Those times were noteworthy for their singular lack of tolerance. Protestant and Catholic dynasties came and went, leaving the throne first in the hands of the "heretics" (Protestants), then in the grasp of the "papists" (Catholics), and then back to Protestant rule once again.

In Fox's native England, it began a century before him with the most famous Henry of all. Henry Tudor, known to history as Henry VIII, had more problems than six wives to deal with during his reign of thirty-seven years at the beginning of the sixteenth century. He also had a revolution on his hands. A religious revolution. Martin Luther had challenged papal authority and succeeded in convincing German princes that they would be better off keeping their taxes than sending them to Rome. Of course, there were deep religious and philosophical reasons for Luther's break with Roman Catholicism, but economic factors helped him gain the backing of powerful rulers and ensured his break with Roman Catholicism would not be quelled by armed might alone.

Responding to these religio-political circumstances and desiring increased status in the eyes of the papacy, King Henry penned a denunciation of Luther in 1521 entitled *Assertion of the Seven Sacraments against Martin Luther*. It was poorly constructed, containing mostly biblical quotes juxtaposed with relentless abuse. Henry wrote of Luther:

> What serpent so venomous as he who calls the pope's authority tyrannous?...What a great limb of the Devil is he, endeavoring to tear the Christian members of Christ from their head!...the whole Church is subject not only to Christ but...to Christ's vicar, the Pope of Rome.[2]

Luther, no pushover when it came to controversy, replied in kind, calling the King a bevy of otherwise unprintable names. Luther's transcendent acrimony made Henry's sputtering assault sound almost affable by comparison. Here is a censored excerpt:

> ...that frantic madman...the King of Lies...by God's disgrace King of England...Since with malice aforethought that damnable and

---

2.   Durant, *Vol. VI: The Reformation*, 532.

rotten worm has lied against my King in heaven it is right for me to bespatter this English monarch with his own filth.[3]

In Rome the reigning Pope Leo X was cheered by Henry's frontal assault on the mega-heretic Luther's doctrine and character. Leo awarded the English King the title *Defensor Fidei,* Defender of the Faith, which Henry received proudly. Later, when breaking with Rome over his attempt to divorce Catherine of Aragon and marry his pregnant girlfriend, Anne Boleyn, Henry would outlaw both Lutheranism and Catholicism. He reasoned that if the Catholic Church refused to grant his divorce, he would simply divorce the Catholic Church and make himself head of a Church of England.

This unprecedented pomposity prompted Luther to grumble, "This king wants to be God. He founds articles of faith, which even the Pope never did."[4]

Risky Topics: Religion and Politics

And all these groups busily set to work persecuting, flogging, attacking with armies, and burning each other at the stake. It was a tough time to be a common man, because you didn't know which side to support or which form of religion to embrace. If you became an Anglican by joining the Protestant State Church founded by Henry and the Catholics came to power, which they did when his daughter Mary took the throne, life got rather complicated and uncomfortable. So, quite a few people converted to Catholicism during Mary's reign, only to find themselves on the outside of the Establishment when her half-sister, the Protestant Queen Elizabeth, took over.

Those were times when a person could be hanged for the merest offense. Burning at the stake was the common lot for those who were found to be "heretics." What was a heretic? Anyone who disagreed with the fellow holding the matches to light the execution pyre. First, Henry was the Defender of the Faith, opponent of Protestantism. Then the Tudor king threw off Roman influence and established a Protestant church. It was a time for wise men to keep silent about religion and politics, a hesitation which survives today.

---

3. Ibid.
4. Edith Simon, *The Great Age of Man: The Reformation* (Alexandria, VA: Time-Life Books, Inc., 1966), 82.

As late as 1639 the British government considered burning a tradesman as an example to other secret heretics. And the pernicious crimes with which he was accused?

> The counts on which he was charged…non-attendance at church, studying the Bible at home, being against printed prayers, and being opposed to the systems of bishops.[5]

The hapless tradesman was not burned, but he could have been. By those standards, most people today could have been toasted at the heretic's pole, had they lived in his era. Into this mad, bloodthirsty religious whirlpool walked a man of joy, peace and boundless enthusiasm, a man who would neither be silent nor bow to anyone but his Lord. His name was George Fox.

"Blessed Instrument of God"

Listen as Fox's most famous convert, colonial father William Penn, introduces his friend:

> The blessed instrument…of God…of whom I am now about to write, was George Fox…a worthy man, witness and servant of God in his time…George Fox was born in Leicestershire, about the year 1624. He descended of honest and sufficient parents, who endeavored to bring him up…in the way of the worship of the nation.[6]

"…the worship of the nation" could only mean the Church of England, Anglicanism, or as it is known in the American continent, the Episcopal Church. During the reign of Queen Elizabeth I, Anglicanism became a state Protestant church which proudly charted a course in the "Middle Way," between Lutheranism and Catholicism. Church of England would be Lutheran in certain doctrines (e.g., justification by faith) and yet retain the Catholic system of bishops and a high church ritual quite similar to the Roman Catho-

---

5.   Henry Van Etten, *George Fox and the Quakers*, trans. E. Kelvin Osborn (NY: Harper Torchbooks, 1959), 9.

6.   William Penn, "The Testimony of William Penn Concerning That Faithful Servant, George Fox," *The Journal of George Fox*, ed. Rufas M. Jones (NY: Capricorn Books, 1963), 50.

lic Mass. The primary difference was that now the head of the church was not the Pope but the ruling monarch.

In theory, Anglicanism saw itself as moderate, tolerant, willing to allow divergences of opinion. To be fair to the Episcopalians of today, one should note that this really does characterize the general tone of the Anglican communions down to this day: moderate liberalism in an open framework, nurtured by ancient ritual and a high view of sacrament and ministry. However, in the days of George Fox tolerance found its definition in a much narrower context. The early Church of England was quite oppressive of anyone who didn't conform to its teachings. These "non-conformists" as they were called, often found themselves jailed, their property confiscated, and sometimes their lives forfeited.

Everyone had to pay taxes. What people in the North American continent often fail to realize is that the tradition of Church and State as separate entities is not worldwide. Most European churches get operating money from tax revenues. If your church was branded "heretical" by the government in power—as were all but the Anglican churches—that meant not only would your group be cut off from any government money to support your church, you would also be taxed to support a church to which you did not subscribe. Your taxes would go in part to pay the salaries of Anglican clergy and provide upkeep on State Church buildings. Protestors to the system were jailed, beaten, and killed.

George Fox did not seem to notice the danger. Born of humble stock in a tiny village in Leicestershire, the young man seemed from the outset to be a spiritual seeker who questioned, wondered, and marveled at all he discovered. He used the quaint language of that era to describe his spiritual journeying, so while looking at his writings and experiences it is important to rethink the definitions of certain words to understand what Fox actually said. This is, incidentally, an equal problem when reading the archaic language of the King James Bible, translated in 1611, thirteen years before Fox was born.

Journaling and Journeying

Young George Fox hungered for some kind of spiritual insight. He recorded his struggles in his *Journal*, which has come down to us as one of the most remarkable spiritual autobiographies ever written:

> I was about twenty years of age when these exercises [soul-searchings]
> came upon me, and some years I continued in that condition, in great
> trouble [distress], and fain I would have put it from me. I went to
> many a priest to look for comfort, but found no comfort from them.[7]

He began his wanderings about this time, traveling on horseback and on
foot. Later, he would travel by ship to spread his doctrine of peace and love to
the West Indies and North America. He was a rugged man, enduring much
physical suffering in the service of his Lord.

He told of a night spent in the Americas when it was so cold that they
made a fire in the woods to keep warm, but a basin of water near the fire froze
solid before dawn. They slept on the ground that night, as they usually did.
Fox wrote in his characteristic manner of understatement:

> That night, also, we lay in the woods; and so extremely cold was the
> weather, the wind blowing high, and the frost and snow being great,
> that it was hard for some of us to abide it.[8]

Yet, those days of zealous missionary activity were still in the future as
young George Fox roamed the hillsides of rural England in his quest for spiritual enlightenment during the early years of his adulthood. He often went to
clergymen for help. But the institutional religion, which had grown up under
Henry VIII and suffered through persecutions by one ruling party after
another, bred men of the cloth who hesitated to give opinions on anything
slightly controversial. George Fox brought them questions and problems of a
deeply disturbing, provocative nature. He could find no member of the establishment clergy to discuss them with him.

He was discussing his plight with a cleric, named Dr. Cradock, walking in
the afternoon sunlight through the clergyman's garden. Reading Fox's *Journal*,
one suspects the seventeenth century Anglican clergy had little training in pastoral counseling:

> Now, as we were walking together in his garden, the alley being nar-
> row, I chanced, in turning, to set my foot on the side of a [flower]
> bed, at which the man was in a rage, as if his house had been on fire.

---

7. Jones, 70. (Parenthetical definitions added.)
8. Ibid., 530.

Thus all our discourse was lost, and I went away in sorrow, worse than when I came.[9]

Pendle Hill Experience

Confused but undaunted, George kept traveling in hopes of encountering someone who would enlighten him. In this, his story resembles the wanderings of Abraham, the searching of Paramahansa Yogananda, or the wilderness period early in the ministry of Jesus. Other great religious leaders—Moses, Buddha, Mohammed, Baha'u'llah, Joseph Smith—had to go apart from the crowd to seek their vision of Truth, which they would bring back from the wilderness to teach their followers.

For George Fox, his moment of enlightenment came on a quiet English hilltop. It was only after five years of wandering—meeting failure and despair, convincing a few people but suffering imprisonment twice for his incessant questioning—that Fox would come to his mature vision of what the ancient faith ought to be. D. Elton Trueblood describes this experience in his book *The People Called Quakers*:

> He climbed a hill on the border of Lancastershire and Yorkshire, part of the Pennine range, and there, on a beautifully clear day, arrived at a wholly new conception of his work in the world.[10]

Fox himself wrote:

> As we traveled we came near a very great hill, called Pendle Hill, and I was moved of the Lord to go to the top of it, which I did with difficulty, it was so steep and high. When I was come to the top, I saw the sea bordering Lancastershire. From the top of this hill the Lord let me see in what places he had a great people to be gathered...Christ was come to teach people Himself, by His power and Spirit in their hearts, and to bring people off from all the world's ways and teachers, to His own free teaching...[11]

---

9. Ibid.,73.
10. D. Elton Trueblood, *The People Called Quakers* (NY: Harper & Row, 1966), 22.
11. Jones, 150.

What was this message George Fox perceived? Martin Marty of the University of Chicago's Divinity School summarized it succinctly: "Christ lives in the inner man—only there."[12] Fox said religious Truth (he used capital "T") must be proven in everyday life. He preached that all persons, men and women alike, have within them an inner light which can guide them, if they will listen to it. He identified this light with the spirit of Christ, which he said dwells in everyone. Moreover, he insisted that it was not in external ceremonies and rituals that Truth could be known, but only through meditation and introspection. Only within humanity does divinity dwell, he said, not in temples made of stone by human hands.

He was certainly teaching nothing new. Paul told the Athenians much the same thing in his speech on Mars' Hill, recorded by Luke in Acts 17:22-31. George Fox, however, had the temerity to actually believe it. He lived his life as though God's indwelling Spirit were readily available to him for continual guidance. He spoke frequently of "openings" of spiritual insights, which he gleaned almost daily.

A few passages from his *Journal* will illustrate the remarkable quality of George Fox's ceaseless communion with his inner Guide:

> Now the Lord God opened to me by His invisible power that every man was enlightened by the divine Light of Christ, and I saw it shine through all, and that they that believed in it came out of condemnation to the Light of life, and became children of it…On a certain time, as I was walking in the fields, the Lord said unto me, 'Thy name is written in the Lamb's book of life, which was before the foundation of the world' and as the Lord spoke it, I believed, and saw in it the new birth…Moreover, when the Lord sent me forth into the world, He forbade me to put off my hat to any, high or low; and I was required to Thee and Thou all men and women (that is, say 'Thee' and 'Thou' instead of 'You'), without any respect to rich or poor, great or small.[13]

---

12. Martin, E. Marty, *A Short History of Christianity* (Cleveland, Ohio: World Publishing Co., 1966), 265.
13. Jones, 101-102,105.

Punches & Prisons

Privileges of rank and title ruled the land in those days, yet George Fox and his swelling ranks of fellow-seekers refused to bow, scrape, or doff their hats to anyone. This managed to offend almost everyone, as Fox describes:

> Oh, the blows, punchings, beatings and imprisonments that we underwent for not putting off our hats to men! Some had their hats violently plucked off and thrown away, so that they quite lost them. The bad language and evil usage we received on this account are hard to be expressed, besides the danger we were sometimes in of losing our lives for this matter…[14]

Dutch theologian Henry Van Etten describes the kind of reception Quakerism received in the New World during Fox's lifetime:

> Persecution was fierce: they were expelled from Boston, and they were threatened with death if they returned to Massachusetts; but they returned. Four of them were executed at Boston between 1659 and 1661; one of these, Mary Dyer, who had been pardoned the previous year, was hanged because she had come back a third time.[15]

George Fox spent time in prison, too. There was a standing order that every English subject could be required to take an oath of loyalty to the King. This oath had to be sworn in public upon a Bible. "Friends," as the Quakers began to call themselves, refused to take an oath because of the teaching of Jesus in Matthew 5:34-37. This led an already critical government to believe that these gentle Quakers, who called themselves "Children of the Light," were disloyal, rebellious, and plotting to overthrow the government.

England had just gone through a revolution and counter-revolution. King Charles I was beheaded; Oliver Cromwell became dictator of a nation without a king. Cromwell's republic died with him, and the Stuart restoration brought Charles II to the throne in 1660, during the height of Fox's activism. An already nervous government, besieged with plots by Catholics and radical

---

14. Ibid.
15. Van Etten, 86.

Protestants to set up their form of theocratic government, established a loyalty oath that all subjects could be required to affirm on pain of imprisonment.

Because the Friends refused to swear any oath whatsoever, many went to jail rather than surrender their beliefs. A remarkable record of such a trial is found in George Fox's *Journal*. Admittedly a one-sided report, it nevertheless takes the reader back to an era when religious tolerance was considered a dangerous and radical idea.

Jail the Bible, Not Me!

Fox was arraigned on charges of refusing to swear the loyalty oath. After a mistrial, he was declared free, but the judge put the oath to him once more. Fox was handed a Bible and directed to swear the oath upon it. Here is his reply:

> Then said I, 'Ye have given me a book here to kiss and swear on, and this book which ye have given me to kiss says, 'Kiss the Son;' and the Son says in this book, 'Swear not at all,' and so says the Apostle James. Now, I say as the book says, and yet ye imprison me, why do ye not imprison the book for saying so?[16]

Fox argued so persuasively the judge confessed that he wished the law were otherwise. He sent George to jail.

Quaker Universalism & "Mom-Mom Quell"

Another element in Quaker belief which caused such a stir was their radical universalism, that is, their acceptance of other people as having the Inner Light, too. Even Puritans, who accepted the idea that revelation outside the Bible was possible, found this idea loathsome. After all, if our Truth conflicts with your Truth, how can you be right? Fox insisted that Truth was one, and yet there could be different viewpoints. He accepted the Inner Light in all people—slaves and freedmen, Indians, Muslims, and all other Christian denominations. "And this I knew experimentally."[17]

---

16. Van Etten, 86.
17. Ibid., 82.

The result of his open-mindedness can be seen in the demographics of colonial America. Puritan New England allowed immigrants, at first, from only sects like their own. Quaker Pennsylvania welcomed everyone—Jews, Catholics, Anglicans, Mennonites, Moravians, and others. Boston had its executions for heresy; Philadelphia flourished as a multi-cultural center where the radicals of another age would guarantee freedom of belief for all.[18]

On a personal note, my grandmother came from Quaker stock in southeastern Pennsylvania, and I grew up in a city designed by members of the Penn family, Reading, Pennsylvania. Esther Marie Quell took her deep tolerance for people of different races with her when my grandfather was assigned to the segregated South during World War II. The feisty little Pennsylvania Dutchwoman, who would one day be known to my generation as "Mom-Mom Quell", refused to treat people of color as second-class citizens, even if it was the cultural norm in Arkansas of the 1940's. Her universalism landed Ms. Quell in more than one confrontation with local customs. One time an elderly African-American man stepped into the street to make way for her on the sidewalk, an imposed, racist convention in some areas. Esther Quell—an energetic, attractive woman in her early 30's at the time—would have none of it. She hopped off the sidewalk and passed him in the street with a nod. I like to think George Fox would have been proud of my grandmom.

The cheerful walker, George Fox, marked the path for all Inner Light teachers who came after him. He denied that authority was external, insisting on the promptings of the Spirit within every person. Fox read the Bible, but reserved the right to interpret it in the light of his inner Guide, the Christ within. His influence and the influence of the *Society of Friends* (or *Quakers* as they were called because of their fervor) remains today. They are still walking cheerfully over the Earth in his footsteps.

Fox found no satisfaction in the confusion of religious sects endemic to seventeenth century England. Like Unity co-founder Charles Fillmore, he decided that in this babble he would "go to headquarters" to look for God's guidance within him. George Fox believed he had found what every spiritually attuned person seeks, the indwelling Presence of God.

---

18. Brinton, 10.

Unanswered Questions

Yet there were still questions to be addressed. If God is in everything, why is there apparent evil? Can a religious system really affirm God's goodness when faced with the catastrophic events of human history? Another European thinker would supply some of the answers. The gears set in motion by early mystical theologians were about to be retooled into an intricate, exhaustive thought system by one of the greatest philosophers of all time.

8

First, Second, and Third Force

Georg Wilhelm Friedrich Hegel
(1770–1831)

In the chapter "Understanding" from Charles Fillmore's *The Twelve Powers of Man*, he makes this important distinction:

> There are two schools of writers on metaphysical subjects…First are those who handle the mind and its faculties from an intellectual standpoint, among whom may be mentioned Kant, Hegel, Mill, Schopenhauer, and Sir William Hamilton. The other school includes all the great company of religious authors who have discerned that Spirit and soul are the causing factors of the mind.[1]

Fillmore correctly notes two paths which can lead to higher spiritual awareness, intellectual and intuitive. This survey has already looked at people from both spiritual routes. The first path leads to a schoolhouse filled with metaphysical thinkers—people like Philo, Origen and John Scotus Erigena—men and women who worked with philosophy and theology to arrive at similar conclusions, including those mentioned by name in the above list. The second path is *participatory mysticism*, preferred by those who make intuition the basis for Truth, like Meister Eckhart and George Fox.

---

1. Charles Fillmore, *The Twelve Powers of Man* (Unity Village, MO: Unity Books), 83.

The names of the first path thinkers are given without explanation, because Mr. Fillmore assumed his readers knew who these great figures were therefore needed no introduction. However, the climate in which the Fillmores did their pioneering work, the latter part of the nineteenth century and the first decades of the twentieth, was a seriously different world than today. This study will examine how that environment promoted the growth of Metaphysical Christianity by investigating the lifework of one of the men mentioned by Fillmore, one of those "writers on metaphysical subjects" whom the founders of Unity assumed were famous enough to warrant no introduction.

Giants in the Land

New Thought is a mature movement within liberal Protestantism, but it did not just materialize from the rare air of late nineteenth century American religious thought. These studies thus far have shown that the theology and practices known today as New Thought or Metaphysical Christianity are really long-standing beliefs of major thinkers throughout the course of Christian history.

Georg Wilhelm Friedrich Hegel was an intellectual giant who altered the intellectual climate of Western society from a sterile desert to a spirit-based hothouse where a riot of growth could occur. When he died of cholera in 1831 at the age of sixty-one, Hegel had succeeded in changing the way most educated Europeans looked at their world. His ideas would find their way to America soon, where Ralph Waldo Emerson and Theodore Parker would give them new vigor, providing an intellectual base for the developing New Thought Christian movement. Hegel did all his work while Europe convulsed in the Napoleonic Wars, and only achieved a full-time university teaching position after he was forty-six years old.

Georg Hegel wrote in German, that erudite and scholarly language of precise phrases, freight-train nouns, and endless sentences. Hegel wrote obscurely even for a German. He is difficult to read in translation and not much better in the original. The vast scope of his philosophy makes it difficult for anyone outside the Hegelian *weltanschauung* (worldview) to grasp what his logical mind is saying.

Coming to the Hegelian philosophy for the first time is like discovering a great, whistling, bleeping machine busily chugging away at whatever it is doing. Observers recognize order, precision. Surely it must be doing something, because there is coordinated movement of parts. However, until discovering some kind of operating instructions or blueprint which explains what the thing does, observers seldom make any sense out of its whirling gears and flashing lights. This confusion is often an outsider's first impression of Hegelian philosophy. All steam and no whistle—and what's the whistle for, anyway?

A first instinct might be to turn and leave, because it will require some head scratching and hard work to ponder the functions of the beast. But somehow the observer suspects the beast is hiding within its form a handsome prince with the keys to a kingdom of new awareness. Hegel is too important to flee from, too deep to wade through, too vast to go around. Students of metaphysical theology must approach the philosophy before them and work at understanding its complexity. There is no other way to understand the origins of New Thought Christianity.

Dominant Worldview

So far-reaching was the Hegelian worldview that its American counterparts, Transcendentalism and Absolute Idealism, became the more-or-less standard philosophy taught by colleges and universities in North America until World War I. Teachers who founded virtually every modern Metaphysical Christian movement began with a Hegelian presumption about reality, even though they may not have realized this embedded theology was influencing their thought. The more effective a belief system is, the more people are apt to assume the worldview is normative for everyone, everywhere. Those Hegelian-based teachers included Mary Baker Eddy, Charles and Myrtle Fillmore, H. Emilie Cady, Ernest Holmes, Nona Brooks...the list goes on.

Because Hegel's thought and the works of those who built on his system dominated their era, New Thought pioneers often assumed people would understand the Hegelian worldview and seldom paused to explain the traditional philosophical position of their time. Explaining Hegel to early twentieth century Metaphysical Christians would be like announcing to a twenty-first century crowd, "There is this thing called *electricity*..." while they were sitting under the lights of a night baseball game. Post-modern people take Edison's discovery for granted, just as people took Hegelian idealism for granted when New Thought was in its infancy. Today, however, Hegelianism is out of fashion, so this study must begin by recovering the view which New Thought's recent spiritual forefathers and foremothers accepted so readily.

Upon examining the blueprints for Hegelianism, some of the obscure passages
in earlier metaphysical writings will become much more intelligible.

Philosophy vs. Theology

Hegel was a philosopher, not a theologian. A philosopher may or may not be a
practicing believer. Philosophy supposedly begins at a point and proceeds logically to wherever truth may lead the philosopher. No ideas are allowed to
stand unless they meet the strictest standards. Philosophy owes no allegiance
to any prophet, concept, person, or revealed religion. It is, in theory, empirical.

Theology, on the other hand, begins within the circle of faith. A Jewish
theologian will deal with concepts native to Jewish thought; a Muslim theologian will investigate the ideas and central themes of Islam. If the Muslim
thinker ever came to the conclusion that Judaism is true and Islam false, he
would no longer be a Muslim theologian. Theology, therefore, is logical
reflection on widely believed categories within a community of faith. Philosophy is individual investigation which may or may not be shared by any other
person or community. (For a more complete discussion of the nature of theology, see my book *Glimpses of Truth*.)

Many early theologians used philosophical tools and were often quite aware
of the contributions of philosophy to clarifying the beliefs of their community
of faith. Hegel is purely a philosopher. Yet his conclusions sound quite "theological" because he answered questions about how reality hangs together: what
is real and unreal, and what part God plays in the study of life. In the language
of philosophy, these are all metaphysical questions.

Hegel believed that there is one absolute power. He called this omnipresent
power by the German word *geist,* which can be translated *spirit* or *mind.* One
can recognize the same root word in *geist* from which the modern English
noun *ghost* derives. Hegel didn't mean *ghost,* unless employing the archaic language of the King James Bible, as in *Holy Ghost.* For Hegel, everything is part
of Spirit. Spirit manifests itself by creating the physical universe. This Spirit
he readily identified with intelligence, Divine Mind. He believed that Mind is
so potent that it virtually creates reality. Hegel did not go so far as to suggest
that the things of the world—chairs and trees, motorcycles and koalas—are
not really there. For him, people see what really is there, but only by seeing
something does it becomes real.

Confusing? Here's an example: If someone firmly believes he is sickly, weak
and frail, sooner or later he shall outpicture some or all of these infirmities.

This is a basic belief of most metaphysical Christians. Why is this so? Hegel would assert it is because people are spirit, and spirit has the power to shape reality. In fact, spirit is the true nature of all that is. Spirit is the energy source which causes everything to be. Matter does not *contain* spirit; matter exists because spirit *empowers* it, much like a movie projector empowers rivers and mountains to exist on a screen. Except that for Hegel, spirit makes not images, but reality. Spirit is the key to Hegel's system.

It is impossible to comprehensively deal with a thinker as profound as Hegel in a single chapter. Two aspects of his system which most directly influence modern thought in general and the Metaphysical Christian theological heritage in particular require special attention: Hegelian monism and the dialectic (thesis, antithesis, synthesis). These ideas are so important that, had he only written on these subjects, Hegel's contribution to religious thought would still be profound.

Hegelian Monism & Theodicy

Hegel was an idealist, which is a word used differently in philosophy than in everyday English. Perhaps it is better to think of it here as "idea-ism." Idealism holds that the true reality of all things is not matter but the power which generates matter, Spirit. Thus it is the polar opposite of materialism. Materialism asserts that the only reality that exists is the physical world as it appears through the senses.

This dichotomy between idealism and materialism explains some of the tirades against "sense consciousness" in early metaphysical Christian writers since it was the materialists who denied that anything could be known that was not known through sensory input. It was the materialists' ploy to deny that anything spiritual exists, or if it exists any ideas about spirit cannot be considered "knowledge," because all knowledge comes through the senses.

Idealism, however, begins with the category of spirit as the most primal reality, from which all matter and energy emerge. Carried to its logical conclusion, idealism—the belief that Spirit empowers all that exists—leads directly to *cosmic monism*, which recognizes only One Presence and One Power in the universe, Divine Mind. However, monism is difficult to maintain in the face of everyday reality. If only God exists, why is there suffering in the world? This controversy emerged briefly when this study looked at the non-existence of evil as a force, as taught in the writings of Pseudo-Dionysius the Areopagite (Chapter 4). Why are there hungry children, battered wives, poor people, victims of war and crime and disease? Could it be that God is not good? An unthinkable notion to all religions.

This problem is called *theodicy*. It may be the oldest religious problem known to humanity, and there are no neat answers to it. Monism, in its radical form, sweeps aside the reality of suffering by denying that anything but good can happen. Radical monism sacrifices the right to feel pain when people hurt for the sake of a theological concept which denies pain exists. Yet, *dualism* asserts two powers, one good and one evil, and is even less satisfying.

Friday Not So Savage

Daniel Defoe pointed out the absurdity of dualism in his classic novel *Robinson Crusoe*. The shipwrecked European instructs the so-called savage, whom he named Friday, in the subtleties of Christian dualism. Crusoe narrates the exchange:

> After this, I had been telling him how the Devil was God's enemy in the hearts of men, and used all his malice and skill to defeat the good designs of Providence, and to ruin the kingdom of Christ in the world, and the like.
>
> "Well," says Friday, "but you say God is so strong, so great; is he not much strong, much might as the Devil?"
>
> "Yes, yes," says I, "Friday, God is stronger than the Devil, God is above the Devil...."
>
> "But," says he again, "if God much stronger, much might as the Devil, why God not kill the Devil, so make him no more do wicked?"[2]

Since Friday is obviously an ignorant savage, Crusoe changes the subject. As a traditional Christian who never questioned how ludicrous dualism was, Robinson Crusoe could comprehend that Friday has grasped something profound. Crusoe's thinking displays an embedded theology. His assumed beliefs which he inherited from European culture included doctrines of evil (hell, the devil, and eternal punishment) and about God (omnipotent, benevolent, with

---

2.   Daniel Defoe, *Robinson Crusoe* (Boston: Houghton Mifflin Co., *1937)*,314-315

a loving nature). Defoe shows us that Crusoe, a typical European of his day, never considered the ideas of God and heaven vs. the devil and hellfire are mutually exclusive. An all-loving, all-powerful God cannot tolerate eternal punishment. No matter how richly His children might merit a little hellfire to motivate them, hell isn't instructive, it's punitive, forever.[3]

Happy-Babble

But the dilemma of theodicy doesn't require hell to complicate God's job description. What about all the suffering which occurs routinely on planet Earth? The presence of human misery causes a major problem for those who believe God is both *All-Powerful* and *All-Good*. An All-Powerful God who refuses to prevent horrific suffering, like the Nazi holocaust, must somehow bear some of the responsibility for the crime. How can an accomplice to evil be called "good"? And if God is good but *cannot* prevent the suffering for whatever reason, how can He be said to be All-Powerful? A less-than-omnipotent God is no God at all.

This, then, is the dilemma. To affirm dualism leaves us without a unifying factor in the universe and makes God either powerless to help or ultimately responsible for monstrous evil, because theoretically an All-Powerful, All-Good God would prevent it all by Divine intervention—by "killing the devil," as Friday suggests. Fortunately some Europeans, like Daniel Defoe, have understood this well.

However, monism in its radical form is unsatisfying, too, because it tends to discount the reality of existential suffering. How could anyone look into the eyes of a mother who has just lost a child to crib death and deny the reality of her loss? This radically monistic viewpoint—everything is *good, good, good* at all times—produces a flow of nonsensical affirmations which attempt to negate the impact of painful experiences. New Thought theologian and professor of religion Paul Laughlin calls this *happy-babble*. Incredibly insensitive to human pain, happy-babble takes the New Thought minister out of the business of pastoral ministry, which is the care of souls in God's Name.

Is there a way to maintain the unity of monism—the belief in One Presence and Power—without denying that anyone suffers? Hegel believed he had found the answer. And even philosophers who do not like his conclusion have

---

3. Stone and Duke, 13.

marveled at how cogently Hegel argues his case. Dr. John Macquarrie wrote this description of the Hegelian system:

> Hegel was not only an idealist but also a monist, that is to say, he held that reality is one. But this unity does not preclude difference. Rather, the development of the absolute spirit involves differentiation, but such a way that the differences are held together in a more comprehensive unity...For Hegel, reality is so much a unity that no individual fact can be fully understood except in its relation to the whole.[4]

Putting this in ordinary language, contrast is necessary in order for one to have any concepts whatsoever. *Good* is the only reality, but it cannot be appreciated unless it is contrasted with its absence, which humans call *evil*. New Thought teachers have long held this cardinal principle. Dr. Cady had said, "Apparent evils are not entities or things of themselves. They are simply apparent absence of the good, just as darkness is an absence of light."[5] Charles Fillmore added:

> Evil is a parasite. It has no permanent life of itself, its whole existence depends on the life it borrows from its parent, and when its connection with the parent is severed, nothing remains. In Divine Mind there is no recognition of evil conditions.... Apparent evil is the result of ignorance and when Truth is presented the error disappears.[6]

How, then, does one explain the evil encountered in everyday life? Hegel has a practical yet ingenious method of incorporating the nonexistence of evil (monism) into a worldview which acknowledges that tragedy occurs. This blueprint sketches the framework of the Hegelian *weltanschauung*. It is called in philosophy the *dialectic* or *thesis-antithesis-synthesis*. In recent years, it has become popularly known to metaphysical students as *First, Second, and Third Force*.

---

4. Macquarrie, 24.
5. Cady, 44.
6. Charles Fillmore, *The Revealing Word*, 64.

The Dialectic

Earlier this study noted that *good*, which is the only reality, cannot be understood except in contrast. Because people have known both *good* and *un-good*, they can recognize goodness. Take for example the phenomena of light and dark, or heat and cold, and the problem becomes clearer. Imagine a world with two suns where there is never night. On that world the people would, of course, have no conception of *night*. However, they would also have no concept of *day*. Humans know daylight only by its contrast, night. The same would be true of heat and its absence, cold. Contrast is not only helpful but absolutely necessary to know the world better.

In other words, heat and cold are not two concepts at war with each other but a single concept producing a third state called awareness of temperature. The same is true of good and its absence, un-good or evil, which produce the third state called freedom. If people are incapable of choosing un-good, they are not free. This is the famous Hegelian dialectic: *thesis, antithesis,* and *synthesis.* Macquarrie writes:

> As development produces differentiation, the differences conflict, but in truth they are complementary, and are reconciled in a higher unity...Hegelian Dialectic, whereby the conflict of thesis and antithesis is resolved in a higher synthesis.[7]

More simply stated by Mr. Fillmore in *Mysteries of Genesis:* "Good and evil, primarily representing two poles of Being, are opposite but not adverse to each other."[8]

Another version of the Hegelian dialectic has found its way into Metaphysical Christianity through the difficult to obtain and even more difficult to understand five volume series on *The Work* (of G. I. Gurdjieff and P. D. Ouspensky), given originally as lectures by Maurice Nicoll. A central concept of *The Work* which has become somewhat popular is known as the *"Law of the Three."* You will immediately recognize it as Hegelianism:

---

7. Macquarrie, *24.*
8. Charles Fillmore, *Mysteries of Genesis* (Unity Village, MO: Unity Books), 57.

Every manifestation in the Universe is a result of the combination of three forces. These forces are called Active Force, Passive Force, and Neutralizing Force. Active Force is called 1st Force, Passive Force is called 2d Force, Neutralizing Force is called 3d Force.[9]

Triads: 1st, 2nd, and 3rd Force

When beginning a project or stepping out on any new venture, from launching a new career to leaving the house to catch a bus in the morning, the energy employed to obtain an objective is 1st Force (thesis). As soon as setting forth, people immediately encounter resistance, problems of how to get that job or catch that bus, which is 2nd Force (antithesis). Whatever the person decides to do in the face of this resistance—persevere, retreat, stand still—this results in a conclusion, 3rd Force (synthesis). The practical aspect of this philosophy is that it provides a way to look at obstacles and forces of resistance while maintaining a positive consciousness. Maurice Nicoll said:

> These three forces are found in Nature and in Man. Throughout the Universe, on every plane, these three forces are at work. They are the creative forces. Nothing is produced without the conjunction of these three forces. The conjunction of these three forces constitutes a triad.[10]

Hegel believed that reality is arranged in these triads. He saw the dialectic operating throughout time, as the outpouring of Spirit continued to create, continued evolving the universe. Hegelian thought is a metaphysical system, in that it attempts to explain how reality fits together, and a practical system, because it insists that truth is known only in concrete terms, in everyday experiences. The meaning and value of "good" is discovered from the experience of the good in everyday life, not from abstract speculation, Hegel would insist. Hegel was also optimistic about the human ability to comprehend, albeit in a limited way, the things of God. In one of the few unobtrusive passages from *Philosophy of History*, Hegel waxes poetic in an ode to Christian seeking:

---

9. Maurice Nicoll, *Psychological Commentaries on the Teaching of G. L Gurdjieff and D. Ouspensky*, Vol. I (London: Stuart & Watkins, *1970*), 108.
10. *Ibid.*, 109

> In the Christian religion God has revealed Himself, that is, He has given us to understand what He is, so that He is no longer a concealed or secret existence. And this possibility of knowing Him, thus afforded us, renders such knowledge a duty. God wishes no narrow-hearted souls or empty heads for His children; but those whose spirit is of itself indeed, poor, but rich in the knowledge of Him; and who regard this knowledge of God as the only valuable possession.[11]

Hegel's contributions to modern thought were enormous. Although he didn't originate the triadic concept of reality—the idea can be traced back as far as Proclus in the fifth century C.E. and before him in Christian and Hindu theologies of the Trinity—Hegel popularized the dialectic and the notion of one unifying principle underlying all reality, Divine Mind. Like a road sign he pointed the way for Gurdjieff and Ouspensky and their popularizer, Maurice Nicoll, who demonstrated how the dialectic applied to everyday life as 1st, 2d, and 3d Force. Finally, Hegel provided German idealism with its most comprehensive expression, which would cross the Atlantic and find its way into the works of nineteenth century transcendentalists like Emerson and Parker, and thus into the fabric of Metaphysical Christianity.

Georg Wilhelm Friedrich Hegel, struggling with great cosmic systems while Napoleon's cannons rolled across Europe, laid the foundation for modern Metaphysical Christianity.

---

11. Georg Wilhelm Friedrich Hegel, *The Philosophy of History, Great Books of the Western World, Vol. 46, Hegel,* Robert Maynard Hutchins, editor-in-chief (Chicago: University of Chicago, *1952),* 1596.

9

The Bridge Builders

Ralph Waldo Emerson (1803–1882)
& Theodore Parker (1810–1860)

Man is the wonderworker. He is seen amid miracles…refuse the good models, even those which are sacred in the imagination of men, and dare to love God without mediator or veil…Yourself a new-born bard of the Holy Ghost,—cast behind you all conformity, and acquaint men at first hand with Deity.[1]

—Ralph Waldo Emerson, "Divinity School Address"

The end of Christianity seems to be to make all men one with God as Christ was one with him; to bring them to such a state of obedience and goodness that we shall think divine thoughts and feel divine sentiments…It does not demand all men to think alike, but to think uprightly, and get near as possible at truth…[2]

—Theodore Parker,
"The Transient and Permanent in Christianity"

---

1. Ralph Waldo Emerson, "The Divinity School Address," in *Three Prophets of Religious Liberalism*, Conrad Wright, (ed.) (Boston: Beacon Press, 1961), 107-108.
2. Theodore Parker, *"The Transient and* Permanent in *Christianity,"* in *Three Prophets of Religious Liberalism*, 140-141.

Rarely do the giants among us collaborate or even converse, perhaps because they have their own worlds to live in and their own spheres of influence. However, there is a record of a confrontation between two great religious leaders that took place five hundred years before the birth of Jesus Christ. It was at the huge Imperial Library of China in the city of Loyang where two men, destined to found two world religions, met face-to-face for an exchange of views.

Lao-Tzu, father of Taoism, clashed with Kung-Fu-Tzu, known to the Western world by his Latinized name, Confucius. They represented two radically different approaches to everyday life. Lao-Tzu was the ascetic, the one who exhorted followers to withdraw from the world and contemplate the divine way, the Tao. On the other hand, Confucius believed that involvement in the world was the way to a better world for all. Two exchanges from their debate will suffice for a good summary of their positions.

Lao-Tzu said:

> "One should contemplate the meaning of death and the way of the divine."

Confucius replied:

> "How can one know anything about death when we know so little about life? They that teach of the gods are often ignorant of human ways."[3]

Self-Centered Religion?

This simple point-and-counterpoint between two of humanity's greatest religious teachers draws a good contrast. What is the goal of true religion? For some it is self-centered, and "self-centered" as it is used here doesn't necessarily mean "selfish." Self-centered religion concerns itself with individual spirituality through good works, faith, acts of piety, meditation, prayer, and other techniques. The goal of this first kind of religion, that advocated by Lao-Tzu,

---

3. George N. Marshall, *Challenge of a Liberal Faith* (New Canaan, CT: 1980), 106-107.

is individual salvation. It begins and ends with the individual, and therefore does nothing by itself to promote the general good of all humanity.

Although some New Testament authors suggest the individual must "seek first the Kingdom of God," other voices call to the followers of Jesus Christ from different directions along the journey to individual "salvation" (Christ-consciousness), e.g., the voice of the poor, the oppressed, the hungry, the sick, the downtrodden. Jesus spoke explicitly about the commitment He expected His followers to show in regard to the least among them. Yet, a long-standing debate has raged between the Taoist and Confucianist perspective in people of all religions.

Some say people are in this life to find their spiritual path; getting themselves on course will soon enough change the world's direction. Others believe anyone truly on a journey to enlightenment will find it impossible to progress down the spiritual path with sick, hungry, destitute people strewn along the way. For this latter group, spirituality is always a call to make this world a better place by doing unto others what we would want done unto us.

Two great American religious thinkers represent this clash of theories. They are the subject of this study, the first one to leap across the ocean from the Old World to the new and deal with theologians who are part of both the American heritage and New Thought theological ancestry. One needs practically no introduction. Ralph Waldo Emerson is required reading in nearly every school district in the United States and studied by quite a few international students as well. He has been called the American Shakespeare, and has the distinction of being the author most frequently quoted in New Thought publications, with the possible exception of William Shakespeare. For example, in *Lessons in Truth*, Cady mentions Emerson's work six times.

Theodore Parker is less known, although his work frequently receives mention in classes on the history and traditions of New Thought Christianity. Parker was a young contemporary of Emerson who knew the great lecturer and essayist personally and who carried into action some of Emerson's theoretical notions.

Like Lao-Tzu and Confucius, they approached the troubles of their times with different spiritual attitudes. Paradoxically, however, Emerson and Parker were not representatives of different faiths but clergy of the same denomination, nineteenth century Congregationalism's radical outcropping in New England, which in the twentieth century would become Unitarian-Universalism. And here it is important to pause to make an important distinction.

Unity is Not Unitarianism: Divergent Paths

Although there is similarity to their names—to the point where members of the general public sometimes confuse the groups—the Unitarian-Universalist Association today has no formal relationship with Unity or any New Thought organization. In fact, the UUA neither classifies itself New Thought nor specifically claims a Christian orientation, even though some UU's affirm liberal Christianity.

As different as these contemporary religious groups may be, it is reasonably accurate to say that New Thought and Unitarian-Universalism share a common heritage until the late 1800's. Certain key Unitarian and Universalist thinkers—especially Emerson—provided theological rationale for ideas which New Thought pioneers would turn into practical exercises. This Lao-Tzu/Confucian disparity pointed to a fork in the road. Those who traveled Parker's route of social and political activism soon diverged from those who continued to center on spiritual growth via prayer and meditation. The former became modern Unitarian-Universalism and, to a lesser extent, liberal Protestantism. The latter, when joined with the nineteenth century science of mental healing movement, became New Thought Christianity.

Although this synopsis has committed the usual summarizing sins of conflation and oversimplification, it does connect the essential branches of the New Thought Christian family tree, albeit not incontestably. This study shall look at two Unitarian clergymen who, to mix metaphors, provided an important bridge in the formative phase of New Thought Christianity. As suggested above, Emerson and Parker also offer a bridge to the past, the long heritage of original thinkers who have caught a glimpse of the divine oneness and passed that vision along to those who have come after them. Emerson and Parker were stellar examples from a century of liberal, New England clergy who, when their work is examined, doubtless will prove to be the missing branches which connect nineteenth century New Thought to expressions of progressive Christianity today.

American Shakespeare

Emerson was born in Boston on May 25, 1803. He came from a long line of ministers and scholars. His father was pastor of First Church, Boston, but died in 1811, leaving the mother to struggle to support the children. Emerson was a bright boy so he attended Latin School as a youth and then Harvard

College. He went on to Harvard Divinity School but never graduated. He was ordained a Unitarian minister and served as pastor of Second Church in Boston for about three years. When his wife, Ellen, died, he resigned his post and sailed for Europe where he spent almost a year.

When he returned, Emerson turned to lecturing and writing full time. He did some substitute preaching but never again held a parish ministry. His second marriage endured the rest of his long life. Although Lydia Jackson Emerson gave him three children, one son died at five years. Emerson wrote movingly about the loss in a poem, "Threnody." Here is a passage, which captures this melancholy time in his life:

> O child of paradise,
> Boy who made dear his
>> father's home,
> In whose deep eyes
> Men read the welfare of times
>> to come,
> I am too much bereft.
> The world dishonored thou
>> hast left.[4]

Emerson recovered from the tragedy, publishing his *Second Series* of essays and fathering another son, Edward Waldo, two years later. Perhaps his greatest contribution to American Christianity came about as the result of his growing fame as a lecturer. In the spring of 1838 he received an invitation from a committee to speak to the senior class at Harvard Divinity School. He was struggling with the concept of ministry at the time, so he used the occasion to air his views on the state of Christianity in general and the ministry in particular.

On a clear, warm Boston evening he rose before an unsuspecting audience and delivered a lengthy sermon which has been called one of the most important Sunday messages of modern times. It was an untitled lecture-sermon which has since come to be known simply as *"The Divinity School Address."* Protestant Christianity on this continent has never been the same.

---

4. Ralph Waldo Emerson, "Threnody," *Selected Prose and Poetry*, Reginald L. Cook, (ed.) (NY: Holt, Rinehart & Winston, 1969), 447.

Divinity School Address

What was the message Emerson preached that lazy summer evening when America was young? He took the themes of German idealism, which emerged from Hegel and others, and gave voice to its American offshoot, which would later be called *Transcendentalism*, applying these concepts to the Christian faith for a scientific age. Earl Morse Wilbur gives a summary of Emerson's remarks:

> He complained that the prevailing religion of the day had little life or inspiration in it because it was forever looking to persons and events in the past history of Christianity, rather than listening to hear what God has to say to men today; and he urged them not to attach importance to miracles...but to seek the truths of religion within their own souls, and to preach to men what God reveals to them there. Thus religion should be no longer cold and formal, but a vital personal experience.[5]

Even more importantly, Emerson insisted everyone shall become what Jesus Christ *was*. He denied the unique divinity of Jesus but saw Him as the Way Shower for humanity to realize its Oneness with God. In powerful phrases, shaped by the finest theological writer of the nineteenth century, Ralph Waldo Emerson foreshadowed the whole vast scope of modern practical Christianity when he spoke these words that night in the Divinity School Chapel at Harvard:

> Jesus Christ belonged to the true race of prophets. He saw with open eye the mystery of the soul. Drawn by its severe harmony, ravished with its beauty, he lived in it, and had his being there. Alone in history, he estimated the greatness of man. One man was true to what is in you and me. He saw that God incarnates himself in man, and evermore goes forth anew to take possession of his world. He said, in his jubilee of sublime emotion, 'I am divine. Through me, God

---

5. Earl Morse Wilbur, *Our Unitarian Heritage* (Boston, Beacon Press, 1963), 434.

acts; through me, speaks. Would you see God, see me; or, see thee, when thou also thinkest as I now think.'[6]

Emerson was already in enough trouble with the more traditionally minded members of the congregation, although by now the graduating students and young visiting ministers were on the edge of their chairs. Having gone this far, the bard of Concord followed his line of thought to its logical conclusion in a searing indictment of the state into which nineteenth century Christianity had degenerated:

> But what a distortion did his doctrine and memory suffer in the same, in the next, and the following ages! The understanding caught this high chant from the poet's lips, and said, in the next age, 'This was Jehovah come down out of heaven. I will kill you if you say he was a man.' The idioms of his language, and the figures of his rhetoric, have usurped the place of his truth, and churches are not built on his principle, but on his tropes [figures of speech].[7]

By now the Divinity School faculty had walked out in silent protest, but Emerson went still further, proclaiming that everything Jesus did was natural, not supernatural. Miracles do exist, but not as supernatural interventions into time and space. Those things called miracles operate on principles of divine laws which are not yet understood.

> [Jesus] spoke of miracles; for he felt that man's life was a miracle, and all that man doth, and he knew that this daily miracle shines, as the character ascends. But the word miracle, as pronounced by Christian churches, gives a false impression, it is Monster. It is not one with the blowing clover and the falling rain.[8]

It is important to pause here and remember that, all his life, Ralph Waldo Emerson regarded himself a Christian minister following a different calling as an essayist and lecturer, what today we might call an *alternative ministry*. He was not opposed to Christianity, nor to the Christian church. Emerson

---

6.   Emerson, quoted in *Three Prophets of Religious Liberalism*, 96-97.
7.   Ibid., 97.
8.   Ibid.

believed the *persona* and miracles of Jesus were set on so lofty a pedestal no mere mortal could ever hope to achieve what Jesus did. It was not the divinity of Jesus Christ that Emerson challenged; it was the uniqueness of that divinity. He believed all people have within them the same imprint of divinity, that Jesus is special because:

> Alone in human history, he estimated the greatness of man...He saw that God incarnates himself in man, and evermore goes forth anew to take possession of his world.[9]

So miracles—supernatural intervention into time and space by a divine agency—were superfluous for Emerson. Those demonstrations, called *miracles*, are natural powers of a Christ nature which all people harbor yet very few display. Yet, if everyone harbors the divine nature, what miracle is necessary, when a person can sail within and find the depths of God? And after finding that Truth, the obvious next step would be to join in community with other seeking souls and engage in the dialectical process of sharing and comparing what has been learned. In one evening Ralph Waldo Emerson had struck down the long held position of even his liberal Christian colleagues, i.e., the chief evidences for Christianity were the miracles and the uniqueness of Jesus Christ. Emerson turned that inside out and affirmed that the best in Christianity shows how very normal was Jesus of Nazareth

> That which shows God in me, fortifies me. That which shows God out of me, makes me a wart and a wen. There is no longer a necessary reason for my being. Already the long shadows of untimely oblivion creep over me, and I shall decease forever...The time is coming when all men will see, that the gift of God to the soul is not a vaunting, overpowering, excluding sanctity, but a sweet, natural goodness, a goodness like thine and mine, and that so invites thine and mine to be and grow.[10]

It is apparent from even a cursory reading of Emerson's talk that he was decades ahead of his contemporaries in rediscovering the nature of Jesus Christ for modern humanity. He challenged others to do likewise.

---

9.   Ibid.
10. Ibid., 99.

Theodore Parker In the Audience

One of the young ministers who came to hear Emerson that night took up this challenge and committed himself to it for the rest of his life. He was Theodore Parker, grandson of Captain John Parker who led the Yankee forces at the first skirmish of the Revolutionary War, Lexington, and may well have been the minuteman who fired that "shot heard round the world." Theodore Parker reported in his letters and correspondence that grandfather John Parker was told by some of the men that they did not like the odds at Lexington—900 redcoats to Parker's 70 patriots. The outnumbered Americans understandably wanted to run for their lives. Captain Parker promptly drew his sword and vowed to run the first man through who even considered bolting his battle line. This action, it seems, was typical of the Parker family, because his grandson Theodore drew his sword-like pen and vowed eternal hostility toward anyone who supported the horrible institution which infected nineteenth century America, human slavery.

Preacher Parker wrote sermons with a gun on his desk, because his home was a station in the Underground Railroad. Many times the Reverend Theodore Parker stood in danger of committing acts of violence even as he wrote words of love. He often had black families in his basement, even though the Fugitive Slave Law made it a crime for him to protect runaways.

These were terrible times for American democracy. Theodore Parker would not sit idly by while his black brothers and sisters were hunted down by his white brothers and sisters. Here is a sample of his vehement denunciation of the law which made slaves no more than property and required all people to help slave owners retrieve their lost "merchandise":

> The Fugitive Slave Bill is one of the most iniquitous statutes enacted in our time; it is only fit to be broken. In the name of justice, I call upon all men who love the law, to violate and break this Fugitive Slave Bill...[11]

---

11. *John Weiss, Life and Correspondence of Theodore Parker* (NY: Arno Press, 1969), 119.

The Lion and the Scholar

Theodore Parker found Emerson's words "...the *noblest, the most inspiring strain I ever listened to.*"[12] And Parker did not simply go home with a head full of new ideas; he put transcendentalism to work in everyday life. Parker truly believed that the divine was within all humans, so naturally he became a fierce opponent of slavery. He saw Truth as one, so he began to study widely and even read eastern philosophies and religious works from non-Christian cultures. He was a committed follower of Jesus Christ, so he was not afraid to follow the path of Truth wherever it led him.

Parker was to Emerson as Confucius was to Lao-Tzu. Emerson was the scholar, a thinker who wove words into tapestries of thought that enriched everyone who heard him. Cady wrote of him:

> Emerson was a man of large individuality, but retiring personality. He was grandly simple. He was of a shrinking, retiring nature (or personality). But just in proportion as the human side of him was willing to 'retire and be thought little of,' did the immortal, the God in him, shine forth in greater degree.[13] (Parenthesis in original.)

Emerson was in fact known for his mildness. He hated controversy and never criticized anyone directly, although he was not without detractors. The shy prophet from Concord had some problems with a minister or two, as recorded in Emerson's journals. One time after he spoke at a church in Middlebury, Vermont, a clergyman came to the pulpit and delivered this closing prayer: *"We beseech thee, O Lord, to deliver us from hearing any more such transcendental nonsense as we have just listened to from this sacred desk."*

Emerson leaned over to the man next to him and asked the pastor's name. He then remarked, gently, "He seemed a very conscientious, plain-spoken man." He said no more. In the face of such attacks, Emerson was gentle as a lamb.[14]

On the other hand, Theodore Parker was the lion, roaring forth on social issues, bellowing against slavery. Parker even pushed for women's rights—*in*

---

12. Wilbur, 434.
13. Cady, 72-73.
14. Emerson packet, unsigned *"Anecdotes"* sheet (Boston: Emerson Commemorative Committee, 1982), side one.

the 1840s! He chided fellow Christians for refusing to do anything about the poor, the hungry, the oppressed of the world.

"Transient and Permanent in Christianity"

In May 1841, Theodore Parker was invited to give the ordination address at Hawes Place Church, Boston, on the ordination to the Christian ministry of Reverend Charles C. Shackford. Parker's speech, coupled with Emerson's Divinity School address, constitutes a rallying point for nineteenth century transcendentalism.

Clearly and in ringing terms, Parker declared certain elements in every religion must be viewed as passing fancies. He affirmed the quest for deeper spiritual truths, which must be culled from the pages of sacred scripture through a life of individual study, piety and prayer. He called his two-hour sermon *"The Transient and Permanent in Christianity."* Even today it reads freshly and vibrantly, a monument to this rabble-rousing genius who pioneered an interfaith approach to Truth from East and West. Wilbur describes the central themes in Parker's message:

> The permanent element in [Christianity]…is the teaching of Jesus, and the truth of that is self-evident apart from miracles; it does not rest on the personal authority of Jesus, indeed it would still remain true though it were proved that Jesus never lived at all. On the other hand, the forms and doctrines of Christianity are transient, changing from year to year…[15]

In Parker's words:

> Jesus tells us, his word is the word of God, and so shall never pass away. But who tells us, that our word shall never pass away, that our notion of his Word shall stand forever?[16]

Parker was refused fellowship by many of his brother ministers because of these "radical" views, which today seem rather tame. Nevertheless, he continued struggling for his vision of a Christian faith grounded in the teachings of

---

15. Wilbur, 437.
16. Theodore Parker in *Three Prophets of Religious Liberalism*, 118.

Jesus but free from the bounds of superstition, free to explore new thoughts in the light of new discoveries of the modern age.

Emerson and Parker built bridges between the Old World and the New Age. They stood at the door to modern life and pointed the way for those who would come after them. Insisting on truth instead of dogma, justice instead of blind obedience, they were two modern prophets who created the kind of climate in which New Thought Christianity could flourish.

Although Emerson is regarded as the great genius, the finest author of his generation, Theodore Parker in many ways surpassed Emerson's abilities. Parker studied and achieved competence in a phenomenal number of foreign languages, including: Italian, Portuguese, Dutch, Icelandic, Chaldaic, Arabic, Persian, Coptic, Aethiopic, Russian, Swedish, and of course the classical tongues of Latin, Greek, and Hebrew![17] An able orator, perhaps the finest preacher in New England of his day, Parker wrote poetry which rivaled Emerson's best verse. The last two stanzas of his poem "Evening" show the deep feeling of this man and summarize his highest hopes for humankind:

> Oh, night and stars! your voice I hear
> Swell round the listening pole:
> Your hymns are praises, loud and clear,
> Are music to my soul.
>
> Sing on, sing on, celestial band,
> Till earth repeats your lays,
> Till the wide sea, the sky, the land,
> Shall celebrate His praise![18]

Ralph Waldo Emerson, the American Shakespeare, and his younger counterpart, Theodore Parker, were two men who struggled for new ideas and tried to live them in the real world. They were champions of the ancient faith who insisted on the right of every person to become what God intended us to be, "a new-born bard of the Holy Ghost." Emerson was the scholar, a gentle giant who tried to influence his world by personal example and quiet reflection. Parker was the activist who grappled with the evils of the day, who led the

---

17. Weiss, *72*.
18. Ibid., 83.

fight against slavery and cried like a lone voice in the wilderness for women's rights, the universality of Truth, the essential oneness of all humanity.

Did they resolve the ancient feud between Lao-Tzu and Confucius? Not really. However, their lives—especially Parker's experiences as an abolitionist—showed that it is possible to be a spiritual person who nonetheless takes an active part in the world. One might say Emerson was a kind of American Taoist who still managed to change his world, and that Parker was a Yankee Confucianist who offered deep insights into the divine. In true Hegelian fashion, they represented a thesis-antithesis which would resolve itself in the synthesis of post-modern consciousness. Although they never described themselves as "New Thought," these two nineteenth century prophets nonetheless made a vital contribution to the development of Metaphysical Christianity. The courage and ringing truth of their lives adds vibrancy and vitality to the whole New Thought family tree.

Now the path of inquiry leads into the twentieth century. The final section of this study will look at three women who launched new ministries which are still in existence today, plus two theologians whose thinking shapes present mainline theology and who may hold the key to new theologies yet to come.

IV

Yesterday, Today, and Tomorrow

10

Three Women Prophets

Mary Baker Eddy (1821–1910 C.E.)
Emma Curtis Hopkins (1853–1925 C.E.)
Nona Brooks (1866–1945 C.E.)

I love to tell of the blessed change in outlook that came to us; of our remarkable healing; of the quick improvement of the financial situation. In fact our entire lives were transformed. We were thrilled! Who would not be![1]

—Nona Brooks, *Divine Science.*

Early Christianity had a sour reputation in the Hellenistic world for a number of reasons. After all, these Christians were notorious atheists—they didn't believe in the gods! They refused to salute the Emperor's statue by offering wine and incense as a sacrifice in worship of Caesar. They were seditious and sneaky, meeting in private cells of subversives where they ate bodies and drank blood in their communion meals. And, worst of all, they allowed undesirables into their fellowship as full members: commoners, foreigners, slaves, and can you believe it, even women! The gossip mills of Imperial Rome mass-produced rumors, and soon the Christians were regarded with the kind of contempt twenty-first century Westerners feel for terrorists.

---

1. Nona Brooks, *Divine Science* (Denver, CO: Divine Science Federation, 1957), 11-12.

121

Actually, each anti-Christian fantasy contained an element of truth, even the allegation of cannibalism. Christians did "eat the body and drink the blood" of the Christ in the Lord's Supper, but not as described by the wagging tongues of Roman rumormongers. Tertullian knew the solid spirituality of the new faith would overcome trendy prejudices sooner or later. As early as the year C.E. 197 he could write:

> We are but of yesterday, and we have filled every place among you—cities, islands, fortresses, towns, marketplaces, the very camps, tribes, companies, Senate, and Forum. We have left you only the temples.[2]

Early Christianity afforded women equal status in the fellowship, almost unprecedented in world history. Even Paul, who admonishes women to follow social conventions and not disturb Roman cultural standards, promotes the ministry of women and heaps praise on the husband-and-wife team of Aquila and Priscilla, two early teachers of the faith. Romans 16:3-5, Acts 18:1-3, and II Timothy 4:19 record some comments of the ancient Christian community about the evangelistic pair.

Abandoning the Example of Jesus?

Yet, the Church quickly lost its frontrunner status in the cause of equal rights for men and women. Medieval Christianity, following the antagonistic example of Augustine, shunned women as leaders in the congregation. Once condemned for its ground-breaking role in the equality of women, the medieval church settled into comfortable old patterns of male supremacy. It was as though the other-worldly theologies of the Gnostics, like the school of early Christians which produced the *Gospel of Thomas*, had prevailed. In that non-canonical gospel women are considered so nefarious they may inherit eternal life only by becoming male.

> Simon Peter said to them, "Make Mary leave us, for females don't deserve life."

---

2. Ayer, 52.

Jesus said, "Look, I will guide her to make her male, so that she too may become a living spirit resembling you males. For every female who makes herself male will enter the kingdom of Heaven."[3]

Other Gnostic thinkers would say that matter is so totally evil that Jesus could not have been born of woman, He only appeared to be. Although the general character of the Gnostic heresies was toward full emancipation of women—as was the teaching of Jesus—the church seized on the worst elements of Gnostic docetism and dualism and dismissed encouraging theological concepts about the equality of the sexes.

Nevertheless, healthier attitudes have a way of bobbing to the surface. If Christian thinkers had followed the example of Jesus—who treated women as intellectual and spiritual equals—perhaps we would have been spared many centuries of men dominating the other half of the human race to its collective impoverishment. A thousand years later, in the development of New Thought Christianity, women reemerged as powerful leaders, pioneer thinkers, and doers.

In this study we shall briefly survey the contribution of three women prophets of modern mystical Christianity. Two founded movements which survive today. One taught more teachers than any other early thinker in the New Thought Christian era. All wrote, taught, and lived their faith. If they had not done what they did when they did, it is quite probable that there would be no metaphysical Christian movement in this century to carry on the work of Christian mystics throughout the ages.

They are Mary Baker Eddy, Emma Curtis Hopkins, and Nona Brooks. Tides of history brought these three women in sequential relationship to each other, as in the ancient world where Socrates taught Plato, Plato taught Aristotle, and Aristotle taught Alexander the Great. No such clear line can be found linking the three, but a linkage of relationships does exist. To explore who they were and what they said, we must go back to the days of the mid-nineteenth century once more.

---

3. http://www.webcom.com/~gnosis/naghamm/gosthom.html, accessed 09-25-06.

Quimby Connection

Emerson is still writing and lecturing at Concord, although his health is beginning to fail. Transplanted absolute idealism of German philosophers like Hegel has bloomed in America as Transcendentalism. Meanwhile, mental healers, patterned after the bizarre Frenchman Anton Mesmer (1734-1815), travel the country performing various kinds of healings. They lay-on hands, dispense medicine oils, and sometimes sell charms and talismans. Most are fakers and opportunists.

But in this crowd of charlatans there is one man who seems to have found a way to make the theories of transcendentalism work in the realm of healing. His name is Phineas P. Quimby. Son of a blacksmith, Quimby spent most of his life in New England and died in 1866 at the age of sixty-three. Quimby believed he had rediscovered the healing secrets of Jesus. He started life as a "mesmerist" but moved to practice spiritual/mental healing without the quackery which had plagued alternative healing methods.

One of Quimby's patients was a woman named Mary Patterson. She came to him with a long history of invalidism after her husband, Dr. Patterson, had written to Quimby at Portland, Maine, asking for his help. This excerpt is dated October 14, 1861:

> My wife has been an invalid for a number of years; is not able to sit up but a little, and we wish to have the benefit of your wonderful power in her case. If you are soon coming to Concord I shall carry her up to you, and if you are not coming there we may try to carry her to Portland if you remain there. Please write me at your earliest convenience and oblige.
>
> Yours truly,
> Dr. D. Patterson,
> Rumney, N.H.[4]

This brief letter, reproduced by Julius Dresser in *The Quimby Manuscripts*, announced the beginning of a new era in American Protestantism. Mary Patterson went to Portland and was eventually healed by Dr. Quimby. She

---

4.   137 Dr. D Patterson, Letter to Quimby, *The Quimby Manuscripts*, Horatio Dresser, (ed.) (Secausus, NJ: The Citadel Press, *1980),* 152-153.

would later teach his method to millions, who came to know her by the name Mary Baker Eddy.

Mrs. Eddy's Christian Science

Christian Science differs from New Thought Christianity on several major theological/practical issues. Perhaps the major difference between the two metaphysical movements is that Christian Science denies the reality of matter, while New Thought Christianity in general believes the world is real but can be transcended by the spiritual element in the human mind, the Christ within. There are, however, more similarities than differences between Christian Science and the other metaphysical churches. The opening words of Mary Baker Eddy's best-known work, *Science and Health*, testifies to this commonality:

> The prayer that reforms the sinner and heals the sick is an absolute faith that all things are possible to God...a spiritual understanding of Him, an unselfed love.[5]

Early in the development of New Thought, the term *Christian Science* was a generic one. Even the founders of Unity, Charles and Myrtle Fillmore, called their teachings Christian Science in the embryonic days of their movement. The term was abandoned by the Fillmores and other New Thought Christian pioneers chiefly because of Mrs. Eddy's repeated insistence that she alone had the right to use the label.[6]

Mrs. Eddy discovered that the Quimby method of healing by mental/spiritual means worked so well that she could teach others to employ it, too. Disease was error; Truth would overcome the false beliefs which caused the apparent sickness and misery. She writes in *Science and Health*:

> The only reality of sin, sickness, or death is the awful fact that unrealities seem real to human erring belief, until God strips off their disguise. They are not true, because they are not of God.[7]

---

5. Mary Baker Eddy, *Science and Health* (Boston, MA: First Church of Christ, Scientist, *1971)*, 1.
6. Charles S. Braden, *Spirits in Rebellion* (Dallas, TX: Southern Methodist University Press, *1980)*, 235.
7. Eddy, 472.

Fierce controversy still rages about whether Mrs. Eddy "learned" her method of healing from Quimby or "discovered" it herself. Her early writings are full of praise for Quimby. But later, as she became the center of a rapidly growing movement, she tried to distance herself from other New Thought teachers by claiming she owed her method to no one but God. Mrs. Eddy attacked in writing some of the other leaders, who often replied in kind. The situation was not very pleasant, and today's rift between New Thought churches and the Christian Science movement can be traced to those early, unresolved conflicts.

It is not within the scope of this work to solve so complex an issue as this. Let it suffice to say that Mrs. Eddy did go to Quimby and was healed afterward; she taught a method similar to Quimby's discovery; and she, more than any other person, was responsible for popularizing the mental/spiritual healing techniques now widely used by New Thought Christianity. It's probably fair to say that without Mary Baker Eddy, we might not have any metaphysical Christian churches today.

Teacher's Teacher: Emma Curtis Hopkins

One reason for the relevance of Mrs. Eddy as a founder of modern Metaphysical Christianity is because she introduced these ideas to another remarkable woman, the second prophet to be studied in this chapter, Emma Curtis Hopkins. The importance of Emma Curtis Hopkins lies in the fact that she was, in the words of Braden, a "teacher's teacher."

> The list of persons who sat under her teaching, either in Chicago...or in one of the other cities where she taught...reads like a Who's Who among New Thought leaders. To name only a few, there were Frances Lord, Annie Rix Militz, and Harriet Rix; Melinda E. Cramer, co-founder of Divine Science; Mrs. Bingham, teacher of Nona Brooks; Helen Williams; Charles and Myrtle Fillmore...Dr. H. Emilie Cady...Ella Wheeler Wilcox...Elizabeth Towne; and considerably later Ernest Holmes, founder of the Church of Religious Science.[8]

---

8. Braden, 143.

It is clear from this all-star cast that Emma Curtis Hopkins influenced most of the major figures in the development of modern New Thought Christianity. Mrs. Hopkins came to Mary Baker Eddy in 1883, and by September 1884 she was editor of "Christian Science Journal."[9] Hopkins and Eddy had a disagreement over something; the subject is not known conclusively, although one historian claims it was because Hopkins began to read other metaphysical books besides the works of Eddy.[10]

Hopkins was a well-read, scholarly teacher. We hear echoes of Emerson and Parker in her writings:

> Your idea of God must not be burdened with the transient and unreliable.[11]

> Write the highest ideas of Good you have. You cannot write a stroke higher than the slave's idea of Good, but you will find that such a practice will pin you down to the truth, and it is in Truth that there is power. All the sacred books of the earth tell that God is Truth, and that Truth is God.[12]

She taught the basic New Thought concepts of affirmation and denial, although she went along with Mary Baker Eddy in that matter had no reality since all is spirit. Emma Curtis Hopkins founded no lasting movement of her own, but her students went forth to change their world.

Divine Science: Nona Brooks

One of those pupils was a woman known to history as Mrs. Frank Bingham.[13] She suffered from a malady which took her from her husband and children in Pueblo, Colorado, to seek a specialist in Chicago in the 1880s.

The doctor told Ms. Bingham he could help her only if she stayed in Chicago for a year of treatment. Dismayed and desperate, lonely for her family,

---

9. Ibid, 140.
10. Ibid., 141.
11. Emma Curtis Hopkins, *Scientific Christian Mental Practice* (Marina del Rey, CA: DeVorss, undated), *36*.
12. Ibid, 37.
13. My research thus far has failed to turn up a first name for Ms. Bingham.

Ms. Bingham was advised by a friend to seek Emma Curtis Hopkins. She did and was healed. She returned home to Pueblo and began classes, teaching the techniques she learned from Hopkins. Ms. Bingham invited the Brooks sisters, Alethea and Nona, to attend those classes. Good Presbyterians, they refused the invitation. Ms. Bingham knew the two women were not well. Nona could eat only a few soft foods without terrible pain in her throat. The new teacher changed her tactics. The dialogue exchange between the sisters and their self-appointed teacher is recorded in the biography of Nona Brooks, *Powerful Is the Light*:

> This time I am not inviting you," Mrs. Bingham stated, fixing Alethea with her eye. "I am commanding you. I will not take 'no' for an answer." After Mrs. Bingham left, Nona cried out, "But Sister, you didn't promise her? We simply can't do it!"[14]

But she had promised, so the proper young Presbyterians scuttled off to a class in metaphysical healing. Soon they were working on affirmations and denials, and soon after that, Nona was healed in a miraculous, light-filled experience. The work snowballed, and soon Nona Brooks was supervising a growing congregation of spiritual seekers in Denver. Later, she would merge her work with the efforts of Melinda Cramer, whose San Francisco based ministry was already calling itself *Divine Science*.

In the mid-1980's the author visited the Church of Divine Science in Denver and spoke with a few the members who remembered Ms. Brooks. They were unanimous in remembering her as a warm, gentle person who nonetheless displayed a strength that came from conviction. The word "motherly" surfaced frequently, especially from Mary Lou Benn, who was christened and married by Ms. Brooks. All knew of her great work, which had reached far beyond the walls of their church building, but they remembered Nona Brooks more intimately. She was their pastor.

Frances Marsh, knew Nona Brooks better than anyone; she had served as Rev. Brooks' secretary. A tiny lady with sparkling eyes and a quick wit, Mrs. Marsh reported that Nona Brooks was a strong but humble woman with a sweet chuckle to go with her good sense of humor. They would sit in the kitchen of First Divine Science Church in Denver, telling stories and enjoying

---

14. Hazel Deane, *Powerful is the Light* (Denver, CO: Divine Science Federation, 1945), 44.

Christian fellowship. The gathering place for Nona Brooks' unofficial staff meetings was a large kitchen worktable with a massive wood top, around which they sat on stools. Frances Marsh recalled Rev. Brooks saying that she always remembered to thank God for her sense of humor, her "funny bone," as she called it.

Snakes on This Plane?

The Reverend Marjorie James told a story about a young woman who worked at the Denver Zoological Gardens and faced a transfer to the reptile section. Terrified of snakes, she asked Miss Brooks to go along with her on her first day, not knowing that serpents struck terror in the heart of Nona Brooks, too. Ms. Brooks reasoned that if God truly is everywhere, He must be with the snakes, too. So, after fervent prayer, she went with the young woman. They fed the reptiles without incident.

After listening to Rev. James tell the reptile story, one comes away thinking, *That is practical Christianity in action.* If there were a central creed of New Thought Christianity—which hopefully there never will be—perhaps it would be the belief that there is only One Presence and one Power in our lives and in the universe, God, the good Omnipotent. This describes the fountainhead of all that Nona Brooks taught. In *Powerful Is the Light*, Hazel Deane records a dialogue which summarizes Ms. Brooks' teaching on One Presence/One Power.

> Someone said: "Mortal mind gets us into trouble and Immortal Mind gets us out."
>
> "But if you want to get well you have to stay your attention on the immortal, the perfect," said Nona soberly. "You'll never get well by thinking imperfection. Perfect God and perfect man, that is the basis. Not mortal mind and Immortal Mind! Not two but One, and that one, God Perfect! Everywhere present! Not two minds, but One, One, One."[15]

---

15. *Ibid.,* 88.

Familiar Themes

There are so many echoes of great Christian thinkers we have studied before in this quote that we cannot spend the time in this brief survey to make the connections called for in an in-depth analysis. Briefly, we hear Hegel's assertion that the essence of reality is oneness, not duality, and that even good and evil are really two ends of one process. We hear Emerson's insistence on the perfectibility of the human soul, George Fox's cry for "openings" through the Inner Light, and Meister Eckhart's preaching that man and God are one. In fact, the movement (known variously as Divine Science, Religious Science, and Unity) of modern mystical Christianity stands in a long line of great thinkers—orthodox and unorthodox—who have continually taught that God and man are Father and Child, one Presence and Power pervading all that is.

The final two studies investigate ways that these ideas have spilled over into the most orthodox of modern theological circles, in the work of two of the greatest theologians of the twentieth century, one Protestant and one Catholic. The writings and teachings of Dr. Paul Tillich and Father Pierre Teilhard de Chardin offer ideas which Christian theology today considers revolutionary, epoch-making, futuristic. Tillich and Chardin are probably the most important thinkers this study will examine, because their ideas are today influencing Christian thought worldwide.

I have a fantasy that shows a host of mystical Christians who have gone to the next world, standing on a cloud (pardon the conventionality, but it's my fantasy) and looking down at these "new" ideas with undisguised delight. Meister Eckhart turns to Nona Brooks and says, "Well, Sister, it's about time, ja?"

11

Shaking the Foundations

Paul Tillich
(1886–1965 C.E.)

To understand the contribution of Paul Tillich to theology we must take a quick look at twentieth century religious thinkers leading up to him, especially his contemporaries in the "neo-orthodox" school. That label need not frighten students of the liberal schools of Protestantism. Neo-orthodoxy was a reaction against the late nineteenth-century theologies which placed undue emphasis on "natural" religion.

With the Enlightenment, modern humanity has wondered about the origins of its religious ideas. In the Middle Ages no one dared question the authority of generally held Christian truth: the Church said it, they believed it, and that settled it. But expansion of European Christianity, both eastward where they encountered a highly advanced Islamic civilization and westward where a New World beckoned with temptations to independent thought, brought long-suppressed doubts and questions to the surface at last. Long overdue, the skepticism at first was good medicine for everyone.

However, doubt became outright disbelief in the heyday of nineteenth century European philosophy. Radical thinkers like Karl Marx decided that God was a drug brewed up by the priestly caste in collaboration with rich overlords for the purpose of keeping the masses in line. And in some times and places, the objective historian must concur that he had a point. However, it is both unfair and inaccurate to characterize a whole belief system by the extremes; a religion is more than individual examples of excesses in the Name of God. Although the Marxist view is tempting, it hardly does justice to the vast cloud of ordinary Christians, Jews and Muslims who down through history have found in their faiths both power for living and comfort when death calls.

131

Neo-Orthodox School

Within Christian thought the battle lines were drawn along a front between those who believed humanity had taught itself about God by what it learned in the world, so-called "natural theology," and those who believed God had reached down to offer a special revelation of His nature and purposes. This latter group became known as the neo-orthodox school because it took the revelation of God in Christ as given by the Scriptures seriously (orthodoxly) and yet made good use of modern biblical scholarship in point to the human element in the writing of the biblical materials (*neo* or new). We'll briefly look at two of Neo-orthodoxy's chief spokesmen

Karl Barth (pronounced *Bart)* provoked the modern controversy which is still raging in the theological circles when he published his *Commentary on the Epistle to the Romans* in 1919. Written in the war-weary days of World War I, his commentary said that human sciences could not solve all human problems, that people needed the special revelation of God as shown in the nature and person of Jesus Christ. To a Christendom which had seen its sons die by poison gases or mowed down by machine gun fire across no-man's land, the message rang like a bell at midnight.

Rudolf Bultmann was the second German-speaking theologian to powerfully influence twentieth century Christian thought. Bultmann pointed out correctly that the Bible is written in pre-scientific language by people who believed the Earth was flat, heaven was in the clouds above their heads, and hell was inside the Earth below their feet. We do not have to accept the three-story-universe of ancient thought to see there is eternal truth contained within the Scriptures. In Bultmann's comments one can hear echoes of Origen and others previously studied. Like Barth, Rudolf Bultmann was one of the foremost theologians of the twentieth century. He embarked on a program of sifting through the New Testament to find the kernels of eternal truth, the *kerygma*, amid its mythological language. Not surprisingly, he called the process *demythologizing*. It has shaped the work of biblical scholarship even to this day.[1]

---

1. I heartily encourage you to tackle at least the first few pages of Bultmann's *Kerygma and Myth* (available at www.religion-online.org/). If you're a New Thought Christian, you'll love it. Bultmann will change the way you look at the Bible, forever.

Barth and Bultmann were contemporaries of Tillich. Barth, in fact, was an exact contemporary since they were both born in 1886. Tillich came to the United States in 1933 as a political refugee after he was fired from his teaching post in Germany for criticizing the Nazis.

Philosopher and Theologian: Criticized for Both

Tillich was both a theologian and a philosopher. Therefore his work appealed to a broad range of people and was criticized from both sides by his opponents. His field of philosophy is called *ontology*, or the study of existence. The older name for ontology is metaphysics, although Tillich avoided that term because metaphysical speculation was unpopular among professional philosophers during his lifetime. Ontology was acceptable, but metaphysics was not. Strange breed, those philosophers.

Karl Barth had insisted that human life must be understood only in terms of God's revelation to us. That meant that even the questions we seek to answer must come from God's activity, not human curiosity. Tillich rejected this extreme, arguing that natural theology has a place, because everyday experience will provide problems to overcome. This commonality explains why certain eternal questions are asked by most religions of humanity.

What is God really like?

Why is there evil, and why do people choose it?

What must I do to experience spiritual renewal?

How can I overcome my limitations?

How can I achieve what God intended for me?

What does God intend for me?

How can I get along with my neighbor, my family?

What is a good person, and how do I become one?

These questions arise from everyday existence. Hence they are *existential*. People cannot go to the Scriptures empty, expecting to find questions and answers like some divine catechism. Human beings do religious thinking as flesh-and-blood people living in real circumstances. Religion must speak to everyday life and provide answers to the deepest questions, not just idly speculate on fine points of dogma. Tillich wrote:

No myth, no mystical vision, no metaphysical principle, no sacred law, has the concreteness of a personal life. In comparison with a personal life everything else is relatively abstract.[2]

That is exactly what we have in the Christian faith: Eternal Truth disclosed by everyday experiences of a personal life, Jesus of Nazareth. With this insight, Tillich built a bridge between natural and revealed theology, between those who say God can be discovered in the world and those who insist that only God can let Himself be known. Tillich replied that God has let Himself be known, and we can know Him through Jesus the Christ, *because* we are in the world that Jesus knew.

Tillich's System of Correlation

Tillich's system sets forth a method of *correlation* between natural and revealed religion. We look to human experience for the problems and questions, to the divine revelation in Christ for the answers. Similarly, Karl Barth is reputed to have said that a preacher should preach with a newspaper in one hand (existential situation) and the Bible in the other (divine truth).[3]

Armed with Bultmann's insights of a de-mythologized Scripture, Tillich set forth to correlate the problems of twentieth century society with the answers found in the kerygma, that kernel of Truth within the pages of Holy Scripture. This is no mindless biblical fundamentalism but a sophisticated system to match problems of everyday life with the answers implicit in the New Testament. It allows for some mighty interesting deductions, especially when Tillich the philosopher is talking. This study shall consider the main points in his theology/philosophy in the briefest ways by looking at Tillich's doctrine of God and his teaching on symbolism. Soon the words of mystical-metaphysical thinkers already studied will thunder anew, demonstrating how closely the principles of Metaphysical Christianity parallel the thinking of Paul Tillich.

---

2.   Paul Tillich, *Systematic Theology Volume One* (Chicago: University of Chicago Press, 1951), 16

3.   The actual quote is elusive and has been attributed not only to Barth but also to Martin Luther, Charles Spurgeon, Abraham Lincoln, Reinhold Niebuhr, and others.

Doctrine of God: The Ground of Our Being

Tillich waded into the deepest quagmire of all, where countless theologians before him had lost their way: *What is God like?* Is God a Supreme Being, an infinite CEO with His corporate offices somewhere beyond the heavens or in some other spiritual dimension? Doesn't that make God just another being among all the lesser beings who exist? Is God personal? Does God have moods, feelings, bad days? Does God play favorites? If the answers to these questions are not forthcoming, what can we say about God that is true?

Tillich correlated these questions with the insights of modern biblical scholarship and existential philosophy. His answers are astounding, if not patently heretical. For openers Dr. Paul Tillich, arguably the foremost Protestant theologian of the twentieth century, declared that *God does not exist.* Now, before we write him off as a disciple of Karl Marx and the wild-eyed radicals, we need to note that Paul Tillich deeply believed in God. He just didn't believe God exists like we exist.

Let's take an example from everyday life. A chair has qualities to it hardness or softness, brownness or blackness, woody scent or odor of plastic. It possesses attributes which describe what it is. But it also has another quality about it that we take for granted: *it exists.* It doesn't have to exist, but it does. It possesses the power of existence. Everything we know in the world also has this power of existence, this power to be. The room you are in right now has walls, a floor, a ceiling. There are probably chairs, electrical appliances, and things hanging on the walls. None of these things has to exist. There is no reason why the chair you are sitting in has to be, but it is.

This equation carries over into the cosmos. There is no reason for anything to be. In fact, an empty universe—darkness without light, energy, or matter—would be more "natural." Yet, there are stars, galaxies of them swirling in inexorable orbits with teeming trillions of worlds where life probably has evolved. All of this is very nice, but unnecessary. Science is an attempt to understand what is. Ontology goes beyond physical sciences and dares to ask, *"Why?"*

Why is there something instead of nothing?
Why is there goodness and love in the universe?
What is matter, energy, and thought?

How do we carry of share these deep beliefs through generations.

Tillich boldly leaped to a conclusion. God does not "exist," because *God is existence itself.* God is the very power to be. He called it the "ground of our being."

> The being of God is being itself. The being of God cannot be understood as the existence of a being alongside others or above others. If God is a being, he is subject to the categories of finitude, especially to space and substance. Even if he is called the 'highest being' in the sense of the 'most perfect' and the 'most powerful' being, this situation is not changed. When applied to God, superlatives become diminutives…Many confusions in the doctrine of God and many apologetic weaknesses could be avoided if God were understood first of all as being itself or as the ground of being. The power of being…[4]

Tillich is not the easiest theologian to comprehend, but when you take him seriously and read slowly you'll find that his sentences are jam-packed with marvelous insights. Some authors give the impression of a tap dancer trying to keep the audience entertained while the stage crew puts out the fire backstage. Tillich reads more like a crib sheet for an exam about the nature of reality. He is deep and wide, far-reaching and profound in scope.

Along with the notion that God is not a being must stand the doctrine, widely held in New Thought circles, that God is therefore not personal but impersonal. For example, H. Emilie Cady had written in *Lessons in Truth:*

> Many have thought of God as a personal being. The statement that God is Principle chills them, and in terror they cry out, 'They have taken away my Lord, and I know not where they have laid him.' Broader and more learned minds are always cramped by the thought of God as a person, for personality limits to place and time. God is the name we give to that unchangeable, inexorable principle at the source of all existence.[5]

---

4.   *Ibid.,* 235.
5.   Cady, 22.

What better description could there be for God as the ground of our being? Tillich never meant to say God is uncaring, unloving, unfeeling. He saw God as being itself, which encompasses all there is, to include these personal attributes. Part of the problem with current understanding of God has come from lack of familiarity with the nature of symbolism.

Symbolic Theology

Some New Thought Christians see all external symbols as dangerous traps, luring people away from the contemplation of Christ within. All traditional "church trappings" are regarded as signs of lower levels of spirituality—stained-glass windows, crosses, use of bread and wine for communion, water for christening or baptism. But what always happens when we eliminate a series of symbols is that another set pops up to fill the need: meditation rooms, flower communions, and so on.

In fact, humans are irrevocably symbolic. We write poetry to talk about spring or winter. We draw pictures and take photographs. We use visual aids and music, which are symbolic representations of feelings and mood. The deeper the religious thought, the more symbolism becomes indispensable. How can we talk of infinity, omnipresence, and omnipotence unless we use symbolic language? Describe infinity. Paint a picture of omnipresence. Demonstrate omnipotence. It can only be done with symbols. Perhaps that's why Jesus spoke in parables and told stories when He taught. He must have realized that there is no way finite humans could totally comprehend God.

The question is not, "Shall I worship the true God or an idol?" The question really is, "Which idol shall I worship?" Which word picture of the utterly inexplicable shall humans paint? Jesus saw that all God-concepts are, and must be, symbolic. So, he spoke and acted symbolically. Tillich made some profound observations about the nature of symbolism as it is related to Christian theology.

> There can be no doubt that any concrete assertion about God must be symbolic, for a concrete assertion is one which uses a segment of finite experience in order to say something about him.[6]

---

6. Tillich, 239.

Great religious symbols spring from rich life experiences of a people of faith. They cannot be manufactured by a Church committee or selected by religious scholars; no symbol will stick unless the worshiping community approves.

Permit me a personal example, drawn from my limited combat experience as a medical evacuation pilot with the US Army in Vietnam. The air ambulance that most Medevac pilots flew was officially designated by the name *Iroquois*. Rescue aircraft buzzed into hot spots accompanied by another helicopter called a *Cayuse*. Sometimes high-ranking officers would observe our rescue missions from a third aircraft, officially named a *Kiowa*. Yet, nobody called Army helicopters *Iroquois, Cayuse,* or *Kiowa*. They were, respectively, *Hueys, Loaches,* and *Rangers*. These soldier-generated nicknames so completely replaced official designations that, if you are a Vietnam veteran, you probably flew in an Army helicopter without knowing its proper name.

A symbol does more than point to another reality beyond itself. A good symbol, Tillich said, participates in the reality it is symbolizing. The cross is more than a symbol of Christianity; it is an integral part of the Christian faith. The cross is a symbol of the One Presence and Power of God. The horizontal bar represents God's omnipresence; the vertical bar shows God's power flowing to humanity. The cross also symbolizes perseverance in suffering, faith that God has everything under control even in the worst of circumstances. Yet for hundreds of years the cross was a symbol of terror and death. Not until Constantine's time did the cross become a widely used symbol for the faith, because in the early centuries of the Christian era, people were still being crucified. It would be tantamount to adopting a hangman's noose as the symbol for the Civil Rights Movement in the Old South.

Killing the Buddha

The problem with symbols is that they are so powerful. If a symbol becomes so powerful in the minds of people, it can literally take over and eclipse that which it is trying to symbolize. The Bible can become God's hand-written document, instead of a symbolic retelling of the good news. The statue of a saint can become the saint in the minds of the people.

There is an Eastern parable which says if you meet the Buddha on the road to spiritual enlightenment, kill him. This cryptic saying suggests even a teacher as great as Buddha can become a hindrance if we rely on him too

Sadhguru never read the Upanishads — Kill the Buddha.

much, if he becomes the goal instead of God-consciousness. That is why, Tillich insists, one must continue to think of God as personal, even while knowing that God utterly transcends the limitations of personality, finitude, and being:

> The symbol "personal God" is absolutely fundamental because an existential relationship is person-to-person. Man cannot be ultimately concerned about anything that is less than personal.[7]

Humans need a good symbol for God that is personal, existential (everyday), and hints at divinity. The greatest symbol for God, Tillich contends, is Jesus Christ. In Jesus one finds what Harvard Professor Gordon Kaufman called the focused God, the place where we learn what divinity is like. When looking at Jesus as a symbol of God, one must do it with full awareness of the dangers implicit in symbolism, dangers which some New Thought Christians have rightly pointed out in the past.

Rich Symbols

To be symbol-free, however, is both impossible and undesirable. What is needed, Tillich contends, is a better understanding of ancient symbols for a modern age. For example, most people automatically translate the "up" and "down" language of the Bible into spiritual terms. However, when the biblical writers recorded and edited their accounts, they took that up-and-down talk seriously. Heaven was up in the clouds, and the land of the dead was down under the earth, as Bultmann observed. Tillich contends that we need to do the same for meaning-rich religious symbols like *God*. He suggests we should transpose images of God as an oriental despot on a throne, riding in the clouds, into thought-pictures of God as Existence itself, the very power to be, the ground of all being—loving principle, caring law, ultimately concerned energy-process in which all humanity lives and moves and has its being.

Even such traditional ideas as bread and wine for communion could be recovered as a New Thought Christian practice under Tillich's concept of symbolism, for what better symbolism could there be for uniting the God-in-the-world with the God-in-me than partaking of Holy Communion? And if God is everywhere, God surely must be in the bread and cup as well. All sym-

---

7. Ibid., 244.

bols must speak authentically to the needs of a worshiping community. Under Tillich's concepts, no agency can select and enforce practices, rituals or symbols upon its people with any lasting success. The test of a symbol will continue to be the test of time.

Paul Tillich's sermons have been collected in a book titled *The Shaking of the Foundations*. His interpreters are legion, perhaps the most famous and most controversial of whom is Bishop John A. T. Robinson. Bishop Robinson published a powerful little book in 1963 titled *Honest to God*, which shook the Christian world in general and his own Anglican Church in particular with its Tillichian proclamations. It is highly readable and can be disturbing in the questions it asks, but it is pure Tillich.[8]

Tillich was in many ways a bridge builder like Emerson and Parker. He wanted to find answers in the ancient faith to the questions of today. He saw a grand unity of things, a simple yet magnificent vision of God as the power to be, the ground of our being. His writings are still required reading for most students in virtually every mainline theological seminary. His vision of God is none other than the biblical picture of God as the One Presence and Power, taught by New Thought Christianity for nearly a century. Paul Tillich—anti-Nazi activist, seminary professor, ontological philosopher, and perhaps the most read and respected Protestant theologian of the twentieth century—wrote and taught in a manner that sounds familiar to students of Metaphysical Christianity.

Saving the Best for Last

The final study shall look at a controversial Catholic theologian whose works were banned until after his death. Pierre Teilhard de Chardin stands in a class by himself. However, he does not stand alone. Like Tillich, Teilhard de Chardin provokes debate and dissent because his ideas are beyond the ken of regular theology. Yet this obscure mystical Jesuit may be the one whom theological writers of the future will cite as the turning point in orthodoxy, the man who brought together science and mysticism for the edification and spiritual growth of generations yet unborn.

---

8.   T. A. Kantonen, *Christian Faith Today: Studies in Contemporary Theology* (Lima, Ohio: C.S.S. Publishing Co., 1974), 42.

12

Faith for the Future

Pierre Teilhard de Chardin
(1881–1955 C.E.)

And he who sat upon the throne said, "Behold, I make all things new." Also he said, "Write this, for these words are trust-worthy and true." And he said to me, "It is done! I am the Alpha and the Omega, the beginning and the end. To the thirsty, I will give from the fountain of the water of life without payment. He who conquers shall have this heritage, and I will be his God and he shall be my son."[1]

New Thought Christianity is not just an integral part of the past and present; it speaks with potential as a faith for the future. This is clearly suggested when looking at the direction Christian thought seems to be headed. The final study in this sampling of "friends" is dedicated to a thinker who offered a magnificent new vision of the interaction between the world and the God who created it.

There looms on the theological horizon a recently discovered giant. A man has walked among us whose views on the nature of life, God, and the future are so profound that some scholars believe it will take five hundred years for humanity to understand and integrate into daily life the ideas taught by this great new prophet. He was not a herald of some radical new sect. He was no

---

1. Rev. 21:5-7, RSV.

pseudo-mystic, peddling his books and offering seminars to eager devotees of the latest spiritual fad. He was a Jesuit priest named Pierre Teilhard de Chardin.

Teilhard—which was his surname, pronounced "tay-*AR*"—published nothing significant during his lifetime except through informal dissemination of his ideas in mimeograph form. His works were banned by the Jesuits and frowned upon by the great lords of the Catholic hierarchy. The Society of Jesus (Jesuit order) refused publication and denied him permission to teach philosophy or be a candidate for a professorship. As late as June 30, 1962, seven years after his death, the Vatican issued a warning in which bishops, religious superiors, and rectors of clerical training were urged "to protect minds, especially young minds, against the dangers of the works of Father Teilhard de Chardin and his supporters."[2]

Today the Church not only has lifted the ban but has displayed a measure of embarrassment that its bureaucrats once tried to silence arguably the greatest Catholic thinker of modern times. A man of keen spiritual insight, Teilhard blessed and released these misguided zealots, and he prayed that he would not die embittered. A selection from his book *The Divine Milieu* suggests he was successful:

> Throughout my life, by means of my life, the world has little by little caught fire in my sight until, aflame all around me, it has become almost completely luminous from within…Such has been my experience in contact with the earth—the diaphone of the Divine at the heart of the universe on fire…Christ—his heart; a fire: capable of penetrating everywhere and, gradually, spreading everywhere.[3]

Science and Religion

To understand Teilhard, one must have a good background in the sciences of anthropology, biology, genetics, geology, physics, and zoology. Because much of his work is technical—Teilhard was a *paleontologist*—this study will need to dip into the sciences to explore his theology. However, the journey will not require complex scientific knowledge, because the result would be a bored

---

2.   Kantonen, 84.
3.   *Ibid*, 85.

reader struggling to make sense out of the confused work of an unqualified author.

What Teilhard set out to do was to provide a bridge between scientific knowledge and mystical Christianity, to show for all time that Truth is one. It was a task somewhat like that which Charles Fillmore took upon himself. The advantage Teilhard had was living later in the twentieth century than Charles Fillmore. He was heir to much better scientific information and an excellent university education, as well as lifelong field work as a practicing scientist. Fillmore's accomplishment was all the more extraordinary because of his educational limitations.

Pierre Teilhard's handicap was formal education. He found he had to rethink everything he had been taught about the *Phenomenon of Man*, which is the title of his magnum opus. Scientific exploration was explained to him in purely materialistic terms. Random factors interacting upon themselves produced random results, moving along a random course toward a random destination. To Teilhard, this made scientists no more than glorified accident investigators. Moreover, it left unanswered some of the most fundamental questions about the nature of human experience.

First, if everything is randomly proceeding, why can science chart the progress? Why does nature seem to select smarter, healthier species over less intelligent, weaker ones? Life came forth from non-life. But it didn't stop there. It continued to progress until creatures evolved who could think. The fossil record shows an onward-and-upward march, from the primeval slime to high tech denizens of the twenty-first century. Is one to assume this is an accident, when a long line of events lead in a logical sequence to a conclusion?

Furthermore, should one assume this is the end of the evolutionary line? Is there a stage of existence beyond our present level of consciousness? In other words, where is humanity going, ultimately? Any rudimentary study of the ages of the earth will show the great sweep of evolution. How can one say, therefore, that all this order, symmetry and directional movement is accidental?

Teilhard set out to integrate his spiritual insights with his scientific knowledge. The results are not always coherent, and New Thought people may not agree with all the elements in his conclusions. However, the similarities between the theories of this scientist-priest and the teachings of mystical Christians like Charles Fillmore are astounding. Looking at these parallels, one must remember that Teilhard is considered by a significant number of theological scholars to be the thinker of the future, the one upon whom vast superstructures of theological teaching will be based for perhaps centuries to come. One scholar writes:

> It is necessary to be Teilhardian because if evolution is as important and is to be described as Teilhard describes it, then certain theological positions which have been very carefully elaborated by Latin theology, and notably anthropology, will very soon be destitute of all meaning. Or, what amounts to the same thing, they will belong to the prehistory of theological thought.[4]

Marcus Bach on Teilhard

Perhaps the first New Thought publication to take notice of the importance of Teilhard to mystical Christianity was Marcus Bach's *The Unity Way*. In that survey of Unity thought, Bach, himself a United Church of Christ minister and religious scholar of wide repute, compared Charles Fillmore's *Atom-Smashing Power of Mind* with Teilhard's great work, *The Phenomenon of Man*:

> Teilhard…was speaking in scientific terms, in theological terms, in evolutionary terms of the identical theme that Charles Fillmore had presented in the sweep and spirit of inspired metaphysics…Someday someone will do a comparative scholarly study of these two books and these two men and show how Fillmore saw unity as being the nature of things, and how Teilhard viewed the nature of things as being in unity.[5]

That challenge must await a more lengthy treatment than can be allowed in a single chapter. But if the predictions of Teilhard's lasting significance prove correct, sooner or later both the secular, academic world and the theological scholars of the Christian Church must notice that Fillmore, self-educated mystic though he was, anticipated the discoveries by scientist-priest Pierre Teilhard de Chardin.

Marcus Bach seemed to think there may come a day when three thinkers will stand out as beacon lights of our age: Ralph Waldo Emerson, (whom

---

4.　*Ibid.*, 91-92.

5.　Marcus Bach, *The Unity Way* (Unity Village, MO: Unity Books, 1982),357-358.

Bach called the "Father of New Thought,") Teilhard de Chardin, and Charles Fillmore.

> It is in these books that Fillmore also reveals his inseparable kinship with Emerson. It is here that the father of Unity (Fillmore) and the father of New Thought (Emerson) would both receive the blessing of Teilhard de Chardin. For Fillmore and Emerson in probing the phenomenon of man discover the phenomenon of God...here that modern metaphysics is challenged to keep step with science and with the unlimited activity of human thought.[6]

One may refine, rethink, rework their discoveries; one can never overlook them. Emerson gave literary and intellectual expression to these ideas; Fillmore intuitively wove a system of thought and action from the best popular science and philosophy of his day; Teilhard took the essence of mystical Christianity and expressed it in scientific language and symbolism. Sometimes scientists have sneered at religion, like behavioral psychologist B. F. Skinner, whose best-selling book proclaimed humanity has grown *Beyond Freedom and Dignity* and has no need for God. With the publication and dissemination of Teilhard's works, some of the sneering stopped. Perhaps his vision is one which all humanity will share when this turbulent era boils down into values and mythologies that can be embraced by our whole society.

Evolution is Going Somewhere...

Teilhard goes back to the beginning. Not the simple biblical beginning expressed in the pre-scientific language of the book of Genesis, but the primordial darkness before matter condensed from the energies of the "big bang" some fifteen billion years ago. Teilhard shows how energy formed into matter, how matter became atoms, and atoms built up into molecules. Ever more complex, ever more diversified, these inorganic structures eventually evolved into primitive organic compounds from which the stuff of life is grown. Organic compounds became simple one-cell creatures, which specialized and cooperated to form multi-cell creatures. From there it was onward and upward to thinking, rational beings.

---

6.   Ibid., 358-359.

This much causes no stir in the scientific world. Regardless what television evangelists may say over the airwaves in their attacks on evolution, this "theory" is so well-established today that to overthrow organic evolution one would have to throw out many of the scientific advances in genetics, geology, paleontology, microbiology, botany, and medicine accumulated over the last half century. A glance at the walls of the Grand Canyon offers a printout of the planet's evolutionary track record that should convince anyone with an open mind.

Millions of years ago, the landmass through which the Colorado River flows became uplifted, causing the river to run much more swiftly. The result was that in a comparatively short period of geological time, millions of years instead of hundreds of millions, the Colorado River cut downward through its riverbed and gouged out the Grand Canyon. Slicing through the Earth's crust, the river laid bare a fossil record that stretches back to the dawn of life. At the lowest levels, simple fossils can be found. As you ascend the walls of the canyon, more complex creatures are always appearing. There are no mammals down at the lowest levels, and no dinosaurs on the top. This view of the ages of the earth establishes that evolution occurred just as theorists said it did. Simpler creatures gave way to more complex; duller brains evolved into smarter ones. Everything moved upward toward its crowning achievement on this planet, a thinking person, *homo sapiens.*

Teilhard goes beyond the limits of ordinary science at this point, for he dares to ask why. Why did inorganic matter evolve into the primordial soup from which living things emerged? Why did more intelligent creatures supersede those with less brainpower? Why did the universe evolve creatures who could question their very existence? In other words, why did energy move to become matter, which moved to become thinking beings?

Omega Point

The answer he gave startled the scientific community, although it does not seem terribly revolutionary to those in the mystical Christian tradition. Teilhard said that evolution is not a random process: it knows where it's going. Life itself has within it a drive to produce better, healthier, smarter creatures. Why? Because the energy of life is being drawn toward something way off in the evolutionary distance. He called that destination the *Omega Point,* and identified it with Christ. Students of Metaphysical Christianity would call it Christ Consciousness.

To the process of evolution toward higher consciousness he gave a new name, *noogenesis* (From the Greek words *nous* meaning *mind* and *genesis* meaning *beginnings*). In fact, Teilhard's works are rich with new terms grown from his fertile mind. He sees all consciousness as converging at some time in the distant future, the Omega Point. One must remind oneself that he is speaking as neither a theologian nor a speculative philosopher, but as a research scientist of impeccable credentials. Teilhard says anyone who looks at the trend of evolution must conclude higher consciousness is the ultimate goal, since that is where nature has most heavily invested its energies. Teilhard even goes so far as to say it is love—the attraction of two elements and their union in relationship—which holds the atoms of the universe together. T. A. Kantonen offered this commentary on Teilhard's thought:

> In Teilhard the passion of the religious man for a God to adore and the passion of the scientific thinker for a unifying principle of the universe are beautifully blended together. On the one hand, he can say, "What I cry out for, like every being, with my whole life and all my earthly passion is a God to adore." On the other hand, the whole Panorama of cosmic evolution moving toward a more and more complex union and culminating in a union of love among men would be meaningless without a personal cosmic center and source of love, God.[7]

In fact, life makes no sense unless something like the vision of Teilhard turns out to be true. Why would a mindless, inorganic evolutionary process move toward higher and higher levels of consciousness unless there were something about the very mechanism of reality which is consciousness itself? Did not another great twentieth century thinker, Paul Tillich, say that God is the ground of our being, the very power to be?

Christ Consciousness

In what direction does Teilhard see humanity going? It is here that the scientist becomes something of a mystic. He envisions a destiny beyond mere physical evolution for humankind. Kantonen summarizes Teilhard's eschatology:

---

7.   Kantonen, 87.

The Omega Point is not in the converging lines themselves but out of this world altogether. Propelled by the love instilled in the cosmic "divine milieu" the unified multiple is moving toward a "critical threshold" where it will make one final leap forward out of the world to the Omega Point. In this ultimate sense human destiny lies outside this planet...And the Omega Point is Christ, the Alpha and the Omega, the first and the last, the beginning and the end. Christ, the radiant incarnation of divine love, not only permeates all reality and impels it toward its ultimate goal but he is also the culmination of the whole cosmic process.[8]

In the creation of the universe one sees energy spreading out in all directions. Kantonen likens this to an impulse bursting forth from the South Pole in all directions northward. When this impulse reaches the equator, it will be at maximum distance from its source. It will then begin to re-converge toward the North Pole, which is the same source it emerged from at the South Pole. When these divergent impulses come together at the top of the world—which represents this critical threshold of Teilhard's thinking—love and fulfillment will catapult human consciousness beyond the converging lines to the Source itself. Individualities will become reunited and one with God.[9]

Yet, Teilhard insists, people shall still be individual entities. He shows that union differentiates, all through the march of evolutionary progress. When a one-cell creature joins up with others to form a multi-cell organism, some of the cells take over special functions like digestion, breathing, etc., which every cell had to do by itself. When people band together in towns, some people can build houses, while others grow crops, and others tend to animals. Union does not make things similar; it differentiates and gives each a chance to do what he can do best.

So in his vision of the ultimate destiny of humanity, Teilhard sees humanity as one with God but still individualized. I shall be, so to speak, that piece of God which is me. You shall be that bit of God which is you, forever. When humanity achieves this, we shall leap beyond this world and take wings of spirit, forever to dwell creatively in union with the divine creativity, God.

---

8. Ibid., 85.
9. Ibid., 89.

While this may sound like James Dillet Freeman's poetry, Teilhard insisted it was the logical direction suggested by science.

Although Teilhard suggested no symbols to represent his vision of our ultimate destiny beyond the physical world, there is an ancient Egyptian logo which might fill the need quite well some day in the future. What better symbol for the leap of consciousness beyond this world into the Omega Point than a winged globe?

Hymn of the Universe

Teilhard prayed for the coming of this kingdom in his beautiful "Hymn of the Universe." Here is an excerpt:

> Disperse, O Jesus, the clouds with your lightning! Show yourself to us as the Mighty, the Radiant, the Risen!...And so that we should triumph over the world with you, come to us clothed in the glory of the world.[10]

Pierre Teilhard de Chardin stands at the door to tomorrow. But behind him in unbroken line stands our heritage in the ancient faith. Men like Philo Judaeus, who created metaphysical Bible interpretation in the first century C.E.; women like Emma Curtis Hopkins and Nona Brooks, pioneers of modern New Thought Christianity; scholars like John Scotus Erigena; mystics like Meister Eckhart and George Fox; great writers like Ralph Waldo Emerson, and outspoken social critics and activists like Theodore Parker; giants in Christian theology like Origen, Pelagius, Tillich, and Teilhard. Heretic and orthodox thinker, rebel, and churchman, scholar and enthusiast—the tapestry of Christianity is woven from the fabric of men and women such as these.

Other Friends

There are other people who also contributed to New Thought Christianity. One could have studied ancient thinkers like Plato, Proclus, Clement of Alexandria, or Theodore of Mopsuestia. Other studies could have looked at medieval mystics like Francis of Assisi, Catherine of Sienna, Bernard of Clairvaux,

---

10. 164 Teilhard de Chardin, "Hymn of the Universe," in *Silent Fire*, Walter Holden Capps and Wendy M. Wright, (eds.) (NY: Harper Forum Books, 1978), 237.

or the unknown author of the *Cloud of Unknowing* or Thomas 'a Kempis, author of *The Imitation of Christ*.

Then there are the multitudes of reformation era mystics and thinkers who could have been summoned as witnesses for the New Thought heritage: Jakob Boehme, William Law, St. Teresa of Avila, or even Martin Luther and Huldrych Zwingli. Closer to the modern age, one could have studied Charles Wesley, Emmanuel Swedenborg, William Ellery Channing, Hosea Ballou, Phineas Parkhurst Quimby, or Warren Felt Evans; and more recently, Simone Weil, Thomas Merton, Albert Schweitzer, Mohandas Gandhi, Harry Emerson Fosdick, Emmett Fox, Dag Hammarskjold, John A.T. Robinson, Martin Luther King, Jr., Marcus Bach, Norman Vincent Peale, Robert Shuller, Hans Kueng, John Macquarrie, Bishop John Shelby Spong, Matthew Fox, and many others.

But perhaps the finest summary of the movement of consciousness toward the Omega Point was written by Teilhard de Chardin in *Hymn of the Universe*:

> Receive, O Lord, this all-embracing host which your whole creation, moved by your magnetism, offers you at this dawn of a new day. This bread, our toil, is of itself, I know, but an immense fragmentation, this wine, our pain, is no more, I know, than a draught that dissolves. Yet in the very depths of this formless mass you have implanted—and this I am sure of, for I sense it—a desire, irresistible, hallowing, which makes us cry out, believer and unbeliever alike: Lord, make us one.[11]

Yesterday, today, and tomorrow, Metaphysical Christianity has friends in high places. Of this heritage one can be rightfully proud. New Thought Christianity is no Eastern religion or occult practice; it is a direct descendent of a long history of Christian mysticism.

What better news could be heard than reports of others who, throughout the ages and into the present, have participated in the same mission to share their insights about the nature of God and the purpose of human life? What better vision of tomorrow could there be than the movement of all consciousness toward the Omega Point, which is Christ consciousness? Until then we who remain in the world can comfort ourselves by the faith which has come

---

11. Ibid.

down to us through the ages, even while we building a better world for our children and the generations yet to come, who will one day literally reach the stars.

Perhaps the time is fast approaching when more and more people will realize the Truth taught by the greatest human thinkers down through the ages: the day approaches when men and women will realize their future is not a bleak rush to oblivion, but a grand reconvening of all sentient beings in the Unity of God's love.

Afterword

Now we have a beginning. There is much work yet to be done before Metaphysical Christianity fully acquires the tools necessary to address theological issues in a post-modern world. The benefits to be gained in such a breakthrough will bless New Thought churches, which have much to learn about their heritage in Western mystical theology, and the mainline churches of today, which hunger for spiritual renewal but shy away from the fundamentalist born-again movement because it fails to meet their needs for an inclusive religious faith. New Thought Christianity is in a unique position to offer its services as a bridge builder. Our background studies clearly show that practical spirituality stands in the mainstream of the mystical Christian heritage when it affirms the divinity in every human being. New Thought could offer its understandings to vast multitudes who yearn for a faith that works in the marketplace as well as on Sundays. But to bridge the gap between our *weltanschauung* and the thought-world of post-modern theology, one must first understand what we share with mystics of yesterday and today. Orthodoxy needs the vitality and insights of New Thought, which itself needs a sense of the ancient church as homeland and heritage.

This study has explored how deep the roots run. It has attempted to find common ground with some of the great thinkers of Christian history. Beyond historical analysis, it has also suggested that New Thought Christianity stands at the cutting edge of the theology of tomorrow. The implications of such a vantage point are clear: those with special gifts have special responsibilities to share the great mystical insights of practical Christianity with brothers and sisters in the ancient faith. To be heard, however, New Thought must speak its ideas competently in the language of post-modern theology. This is the driving force behind these surveys in mystical theology through the study of mystical theologians.

Obiter Dictum

And now permit me an *obiter dictum* to this brief survey:

I see a Christian faith emerging in the twenty-first century that is conscious of its past and active in the world today. I see groups and churches dedicated to affirmative prayer and meditation springing up in all the denominations of Christianity's great family of faiths. I see a new surge in the eternal, upward struggle toward Christ consciousness, prompted by the longing of people for a taste of God's presence in their increasingly complex, computer-enhanced lives. I see world spiritual consciousness, replacing ethnocentric race consciousness, when people begin to see themselves as citizens of one world/ nation and begin to feel that their first loyalties are and ought to be toward the divine Spirit within people everywhere. I see freedom spreading its blessings of spiritual liberty across the face of our world. I see one people, the human race, worshiping One Presence and One Power, God, the good omnipotent.

I see humanity's destiny in this existence as one of exploration, learning, and growth. We look up at the stars and long for their beauty, because the Divine within us knows our future is beyond this lovely, limited world. Our descendents will raise temples on distant planets; our destiny is upward, outward, and onward, always onward, both spiritually and physically. And, if you will also permit me a bit more wishful affirmation, I see the New Thought Christian community smiling as it rallies humanity forward toward exploration of inner and outer space—knowing where we came from, knowing where we find ourselves, excited about where we are going.

Dreams of utopia? Hardly. There will be no utopia until all sentient beings are fully aware of their oneness with God, and frankly that may take quite some time. But if the driving, compelling, overpowering passion of the human family becomes the upward quest for political, social, and spiritual unity in the freedom that God has intended for all the star-stuff children of the Big Bang, perhaps this world will become a little more like an outpost of the kingdom of heaven. I dream of the day when all humanity chants the great prayer of James Dillet Freeman as a testimony to its hopes for oneness:

The light of God surrounds us;
The love of God enfolds us,
The power of God protects us;
The presence of God watches over us.
Wherever we are, God is!

When New Thought Christianity becomes fully aware of the role it shall play in the future of humanity, that day might come sooner than expected.

Selected Bibliography

Anderson, George W. "The History of Biblical Interpretation," in *The Interpreter's One Volume Commentary on the Bible*, Charles M. Laymon, ed. Nashville, TN: Abingdon, 1971.

Ayer, Joseph Cullen Jr. *A Source Book for Ancient Church History*. NY: Charles Scribner's Sons, 1913.

Bach, Marcus. *The Unity Way*. Unity Village, MO: Unity Books, 1982.

Borgen, Peder and Kare Fuglseth and Roald Skasten. *The Philo Index: A Complete Word Index to the Writings of Philo of Alexandria*. Grand Rapids, MI: Wm. B. Eerdman's Publishing Company, 2000.

Braden, Charles S. *Spirits in Rebellion*. Dallas, TX: Southern Methodist University Press, 1980.

Brinton, Howard H. *The Religion of George Fox*. Lebanon, PA: Pendle Hill, 1968.

Brooks, Nona. *Divine Science*. Denver, CO: Divine Science Federation, 1957.

Butterworth, G. W. trans. *On First Principles*. NY: Harper Torchbooks, 1966.

Cady, H. Emilie. *Lessons in Truth*. Unity Village, MO: Unity Books.

Capps, Walter Holden and Wendy M. Wright, eds. *Silent Fire*. San Francisco: Harper Forum Books, 1978.

Colledge, Edmund and Bernard McGinn, trans. *Meister Eckhart, Classics of Western Spirituality*. NY: Paulist Press, 1981.

Cook, Reginald L., ed. *Selected Prose and Poetry*. NY: Holt, Rinehart & Winston, 1969.

Deane, Hazel. *Powerful is the Light*. Denver, CO: Divine Science Federation, 1945.

Defoe, Daniel. *Robinson Crusoe*. Boston: Houghton Mifflin Co., 1937.

Dresser, Horatio, ed. *The Quimby Manuscripts*. Secausus, NJ: The Citadel Press, 1980.

Durant, Will. *The Story of Civilization, Vol. IV, The Age of Faith*. NY: Simon & Schuster, 1950.

Eddy, Mary Baker. *Science and Health*. Boston, MA: First Church of Christ, Scientist, 1971.

Ehrman, Bart D. *Lost Christianities*. NY: Oxford University Press, 2003.

Fillmore, Charles. *The Metaphysical Bible Dictionary*. Unity Village, MO: Unity Books, 1942.

_____*The Revealing Word*, 1979.

_____*Atom-Smashing Power of Mind*, 1949.

_____*Mysteries of Genesis*, 1936.

_____*Talks on Truth*, 1934.

_____*The Twelve Powers of Man*, 1930.

Fox, Matthew. *Passion for Creation: The Earth-Honoring Spirituality of Meister Eckhart*. Rochester, VT: Inner Traditions, 2000.

Greenfield, Jonas C. "The History of Israel, Part I," in *The Interpreter's One Volume Commentary on the Bible*.

Greer, Rowan A., ed. *Origen*. NY: Paulist Press, 1979.

Hegel, Georg Wilhelm Friedrich. *The Philosophy of History, Great Books of the Western World, Vol. 46, Hegel.* Robert Maynard Hutchins, editor-in-chief. Chicago: University of Chicago, 1952.

Hopkins, Emma Curtis. *Scientific Christian Mental Practice.* Marina del Rey, CA: DeVorss.

Hunt, Dave. *Occult Invasion.* Eugene, OR: Harvest House Publishers, 1998.

Johnson, Paul. *A History of Christianity.* NY: Atheneum, 1980.

Penn, William. "The Testimony of William Penn Concerning That Faithful Servant, George Fox" in *The Journal of George Fox.* Rufas M. Jones, ed. NY: Capricorn Books, 1963.

Lardie, Debra. *The Concise Dictionary of the Occult and New Age.* Grand Rapids, MI: Kregel Publications, 2000.

Mack, Burton. *Who Wrote the New Testament?* SF: Harper Collins, 1995.

McGiffert, Arthur Cushman. *A History of Christian Thought,* Vol. I. NY: Charles Scribner's Sons, 1932.

_____ A *History* of *Christian Thought, Vol. II,* 1933.

Macquarrie, John. *Twentieth Century Religious Thought.* London: SCM Press, 1971.

Marshall, George N. *Challenge of a Liberal Faith.* New Canaan, CT: 1980.

Marty, Martin, E. *A Short History of Christianity.* Cleveland, Ohio: World Publishing Co., 1966.

Wilbur, Earl Morse. *Our Unitarian Heritage.* Boston, Beacon Press, 1963.

Nicoll, Maurice. *Psychological Commentaries on the Teaching of G. L Gurdjieff and D. Ouspensky,* Vol. I. London: Stuart & Watkins, 1970.

Rolt, C. E., trans. *Dionysius the Areopagite.* NY: The Macmillan Co., 1951.

Runes, Dagobert D., ed. *Treasury of World Philosophy*. Patterson, NJ: Little-field, Adams & Co., 1959.

Payne Robert. *The Horizon Book of Ancient Rome*. NY: American Heritage, 1966.

Sandmel, Samuel. *Philo of Alexandria*. NY: Oxford University Press, 1979.

Simon, Edith. *The Great Age of Man: The Reformation*. Alexandria, VA: Time-Life Books, Inc., 1966.

Smart, James D. *The Strange Silence of the Bible in the Church*. Phila.: West-minster Press, 1970.

Smith, Jonathan Z., ed. *HarperCollins Dictionary of Religion*. San Francisco: HarperCollins, 1995..

Stone, Howard and J.O. Duke. *How to Think Theologically*, Second Edition. Minneapolis, MN: Fortress Press, 2006.

James, M.R. *The Apocryphal New Testament*. London: Oxford University Press, 1966.

Kantonen, T. A. *Christian Faith Today: Studies in Contemporary Theology*. Lima, Ohio: C.S.S. Publishing Co., 1974.

Spong, John Shelby. *Why Christianity Must Change or Die*. SF: Harper Collins, 1998.

Tillich, Paul. *A History of Christian Thought*. NY: Simon & Schuster, 1968.

_____*Systematic Theology Volume One*. Chicago: University of Chicago Press, 1951.

Trueblood, D. Elton. *The People Called Quakers*. NY: Harper & Row, 1966.

Van Etten, Henry. *George Fox and the Quakers*. E. Kelvin Osborn, trans. NY: Harper Torchbooks, 1959.

Weiss, John. *Life and Correspondence of Theodore Parker*. NY: Arno Press, 1969.

Winston, David. *Philo of Alexandria*. NY: Paulist Press, 1981.

Wright, Conrad, ed. *Three Prophets of Religious Liberalism*. Boston: Beacon Press, 1961.

APPENDIX A

Why We're Not A Cult:

An Unapologetic Apologia for Twenty-First Century New Thought Christianity

All right, let's put our cards on the table. You and I have both heard people say, *"You're a member of a cult!"* and not in a very friendly way. Books churned out by conservative Christian publishers list the nefarious "cults" threatening the souls of believers today; groups well known and loved are usually prominently featured on the blacklist—Unity, Religious Science, and Christian Science are regularly labeled cultic institutions luring the faithful to perdition.

Frankly, when I hear someone remark—*"You're a cult!"*—I want to reply two ways. First, the theologian in me wants to scream: *No way!* The Association of Unity Churches International is a Protestant Christian denomination with roots in the New Thought/Transcendentalist heritage, part of a movement flowing from the Judeo-Christian tradition, grounded in historical antecedents that go back to the days of the Bible and earlier. Why, calling us a cult is like labeling Mother Teresa, Hassidic rabbis, Pentecostal ministers, and priests of the Greek Orthodox Church as members of a cult!

However, when the social scientist in me hears *"You're a cult!"* I merely want to say dryly, *"And your point is…?"* Because the best definition of the word *cult* from a sociological point of view is "…a collective veneration or worship, in anticipation of bettering life in this world or the next, in which the collectivity is defined and unified by its common devotional practice."[1]

So, according to this expansive, social science definition, the answer flip-flops: Yes, technically—Mother Teresa, Hassidic rabbis, Pentecostal ministers, Greek Orthodox priests and the people of the Association of Unity Churches International are all members of a cult. So are Southern Baptists, United Methodists, Lutherans, Presbyterians, Church of England Anglicans, Sunni and Shiite Muslims, Japanese Shintoists, Tibetan Buddhists, and the whole Roman Catholic Church from Pope to parishioners!

We wouldn't be having this conversation if most people understood the social science model of what constitutes a cult. However, the general use of the term in our culture is to whack down groups that are not considered orthodox enough by whomever swings the hammer of name-calling. They employ an erroneous, secondary definition:

> Groups that have departed from religiously or socially sanctioned practice or belief are properly designated as sects (sectarianism), a designation often confused with cult in contemporary usage. In these cases, cult is most often employed as a pejorative label for new religions.[2]

To answer this charge, of being a "new religion" and a non-Christian sect, one needs to examine the best arguments against New Thought Christianity and be able to show why these charges are totally spurious. Fairness requires the faithful reproduction of the crux of the arguments against us, which will also provide a better starting point to respond to the charges leveled against New Thought today. However, when examining the rather bizarre accusations of the cult-hunters, you may find it difficult to believe that anyone could make these claims with a straight face.

All The Interesting Groups—And The Pope, Too?

At first glance, today's anti-cult literature gives the impression that all the interesting groups and individuals have made the enemies list, including the follow mixed bag of 'evil-doers' and their organizations: the Church of Jesus Christ of Latter-Day Saints (Mormons), the late singer-songwriter John Den-

---

1. *HarperCollins Dictionary of Religion*, Jonathan Z. Smith, ed., (San Francisco: HarperCollins, 1995), 297.
2. *Ibid., 298.*

ver, the Jehovah's Witnesses, Maharishi Mahesh Yogi (who founded Transcendental Meditation), WICCA, Hare Khrisna, spiritualist Arthur Ford, the Unification Church (so-called "Moonies"), actress Shirley MacLaine, Theosophy, the Baha'i Faith, the Unitarian-Universalist Association, and Marilyn Ferguson (author of *The Aquarian Conspiracy*).

But a deeper look discovers that not only liberal, post-modernist or "New Age" groups are held up as Satanic Agents. One anti-cult author says he has written to alert Christians "*...that we are in the midst of an accelerating occult seduction of both the secular world and the church.*"[3]

Like the Sirens who wailed sweet songs to lure Odysseus's sailors to the rocks of doom, evil ones are apparently loose in the world, masquerading as angels of light, beckoning true believers away from the straight and narrow. According to cult-hunters, this occult enticement issues from the lips and publishing presses of organizations and individuals so diverse that you will doubtless think I am misrepresenting the scope of their accusations, or that I made up the list up to ridicule the anti-cultist viewpoint. I assure you—this partial inventory is faithfully drawn from an anti-occult volume issued by a major "Christian" publisher in 1998; it represents only a tiny selection of those whom the cult-busters castigate as dupes of the Devil. (Please try to read without laughing aloud, as you'll lose your place and miss some really good ones.)

Beware of the following "occult" purveyors: Alcoholic's Anonymous (the "Higher Power" of AA is Satan, of course),[4] Star Wars movies, the Roman Catholic Mass (called "*a form of magic*"),[5] Charles Darwin's writings and virtually all biologists and geneticists after him, the Seventh Day Adventists, Deepak Chopra, *Christianity Today Magazine*, Sir John Templeton, the United Nations World Health Organization (for approving "*witchcraft under the popular euphemism of 'traditional medicine' or 'native cures'*"),[6] astronomer Carl Sagan (for teaching evolution and that life probably exists on other worlds), Michael Jordan (yes, even Michael makes the list, for saying he's received "*spiritual input*" from his father, murdered in 1993),[7] Native Ameri-

---

3. Dave Hunt, *Occult Invasion* (Eugene, OR: Harvest House Publishers, 1998).
4. Ibid., 289
5. *Ibid.*, 425.
6. Ibid., 133.
7. Ibid., 382.

cans (they *still pray to the trees and rocks and other inanimate objects*),[8] Jesuit theologian Pierre Teilhard de Chardin, the ecumenical Moral ReArmament Movement including *"Up With People"* (founded by a Lutheran pastor who wanted to promote *"consciousness raising and sensitivity"*—shame on him!),[9] former Vice President Al Gore (who *"though a Southern Baptist, worships the mother goddess Gaia and advocates 'reliance on a Higher Power'"*),[10] Sigmund Freud, Robert Shuller, Norman Vincent Peale, the World Council of Churches (for honoring the female aspects of God), the Dalai Lama, and the actress Della Reese, who is also a New Thought Christian minister affiliated with Johnnie Colemon's Universal Foundation for Better Living).[11]

Breath-Taking Narrow-Mindedness...

Of course, all New Thought organizations are high on the list of sinners:

> New Thought was the forerunner of today's New Age, which has popularized the same delusion under new labels. New Thought was forced out of mainstream Christianity and became the basis for a number of cults, which include (in addition to Christian Science) Unity School of Christianity and the Church of Religious Science...

And again:

> The Mind Science cults such as Christian Science, Science of Mind, Religious Science, and Unity School of Christianity openly embrace the occult.[12]

The cult-busters describe New Thought's theology:

> Having reduced God to a Universal Principle that can be utilized according to scientific laws, the creature has become the Creator![13]

---

8. Ibid., 135.
9. Ibid., 300.
10. Ibid., 10.
11. Ibid., 197.
12. Ibid., 116-117.
13. Ibid., 567.

Evidently, one of our unforgivable sins has been to believe that God is greater than a Personal Being could ever be, and that God functions according to Spiritual Principles which, properly understood, are descriptive of what God is like. The Unity School of Christianity frequently gets singled out for special scorn, perhaps because of its extensive readership. According to the *Concise Dictionary of the Occult and New Age*, Unity has "wide acceptance and popularity, even among orthodox Christians who often have only a vague idea of its actual doctrines."[14]

Actually, Unity doesn't have any *doctrines*. Unity people share a broad consensus about a few fundamentals—like God is One Presence/One Power, God is Absolute Good, humans have a divine nature, etc.—but when it comes to the juicy specifics we enjoy an ongoing dialogue about plenty of theological issues. Unity co-founder Charles Fillmore not only insisted on the right to change his mind, he actively encouraged students to find the best answer which works for them. If that model seems cultic to the Religious Right, they might do well to study the teaching attitude of Jesus, who frequently asked as many questions as he answered and seemed to have a high tolerance for diversity. Does he belong on the list, too?

Apparently, we're in good company on the Satan's Little Helpers list. Even the venerable Saint Augustine gets a spot on the *no-no* roster. He is accused of being "one of the fathers of the Roman Catholic Church" and someone whom the rabid anti-occultists darkly suspect as secretly pushing the pagan view of a self-contained world that runs itself instead of the miraculous world pictured in the Bible.[15] In fact, all Roman Catholic thinkers are automatically thrown into the same mix as black magicians, Satanists and child-molesters: all Catholic priests are considered to be in varying degrees of collusion with demonic forces to prevent souls from being saved. This blatant anti-Catholicism in anti-cult literature is not accidental but represents fundamentalist theology at its lowest ebb.

Sometimes, the rhetoric becomes excruciating to the post-modern mind. Take, for example, the widely acclaimed and much beloved Nobel Prize winner, the late Mother Teresa of Calcutta. Although they acknowledge her good

---

14. Debra Lardie, *The Concise Dictionary of the Occult and New Age* (Grand Rapids, MI: Kregel Publications, 2000), 270.
15. Hunt, p. 111.

works in ministering to the poor, dying homeless of India, cult-hunters find that of secondary importance.

> The whole world knows of that sacrificial service and admired her for picking derelicts from the gutters of Calcutta and elsewhere to care for them. But what a tragedy that these pitiful creatures were then launched from a clean bed into a Christless eternity without being told the gospel which alone could save them! It is a gospel which Mother Teresa, as a lifelong Catholic, sadly, didn't know.[16]

Cult-busters delight in proclaiming their exclusive access to God. Heaven has no place for Hindus, Jews, Muslims, Catholics, Mormons—*Halleluiah! Nobody is saved but us.* Does this sound like the faith of Jesus? Where is the *imago Dei,* the image of God, within each person?

Some anti-occultists are even hardy enough to attack the ultimate icon of American Protestantism, Billy Graham, because the evangelist spoke openly of his admiration for Mormons, the Pope, former Israeli leader Yitzhak Rabin, and Senator Hillary Clinton.

> Sadly, Billy Graham himself, though he has faithfully preached the gospel and many people have been saved as a result, has also betrayed the gospel...On the Larry King Live television program...his disturbing ecumenism (even approving of Mormonism!) was revealed.[17]

Such breath-taking narrow-mindedness does not deserve a formal refutation. Religious bigotry is an insult to Jesus Christ, and those who practice it are unqualified to speak in his name. God loves all of us, regardless of how we order our thinking about the Cosmos. The much-quoted poem *"Outwitted"* by Edwin Markham (1852-1940), who was a frequent guest of the Fillmores at Unity Village, remains the only appropriate reply to those who want to damn everyone who doesn't think like them or follow God in their footsteps:

16. Ibid., 577.
17. *Ibid.,* 587.

Outwitted
by Edwin Markham

He drew a circle to shut me out.
Heretic, rebel; a thing to flout.
But love and I had the wit to win.
We drew a circle that took him in.[18]

Talking Points

So far, we have staked out the extreme nature of anti-cult literature. Frankly, most people would not believe the horrific thinking that drives these modern day Inquisitionists. One way to respond to the charges of the fright brigade would be to conduct an in-depth analysis of their bankrupted theology. However, the purpose of this brief treatise is not to bust the cult-busters—they'll self-destruct in due time. This study aims to set the record straight. In this regard, Metaphysical Churches have a twofold obligation:

1. To understand who we are, and

2. To affirm quietly the nature of our beliefs and solid foundation within the circle of Christian faith.

Consequently, we shall now respond to the major objections to New Thought Christianity, which have led some zealots to attempt at draw the circle that shuts us out. Instead of listing the indictments against us *("New Thought Christianity is un-Christian!")* we'll proceed by declaring the truth in a positive affirmation *(New Thought Christianity Is Distinctly Christian!")*.

1. New Thought Christianity is distinctly Christian.

Without a doubt, God has spoken to humanity through other religions. However, a progressive and open-minded form of Christianity is the one that works for us. We follow Jesus Christ because he knows where to go. The Master Teacher, he never demanded that all individuals understand his teachings

---

18. Edwin Markham, *"Outwitted"* available at multiple sites online

the same way in order to be bona fide members of the Christian fellowship. It was only after the Church tried to get organized that Paul and others started proclaiming that "other gospels" would not be tolerated. It's important to note that, when Paul said this, there were no gospels yet in written form. The "good news" of Jesus was open to many interpretations, and it has remained flexible since the first days of the Faith.

A Hindu once remarked to me, "You Christians all agree on Jesus Christ. You simply cannot agree on how to follow him." The way we answer that question—*How shall we follow Jesus?*—determines what kind of Christian expression will emerge. Catholic theologian Hans Kueng—whom the anti-cultists would immediately dismiss because of his papist connection, although he was reprimanded by the Catholic Church for his liberalism, to the delight of his admirers—has said that a Christian is someone for whom Jesus of Nazareth is *decisive*. If you look to Jesus the Christ for a window into what it means to be fully divine and fully human, you are a Christian. Everything else is commentary.

2. We are an historic expression of Christian thought.

Let's get clear about one point: There has NEVER been anything approaching unanimous agreement among Christian believers about what the faith means, what the essence of the message of Jesus was, and how to apply it in everyday life. There is solid historical evidence that the primitive Christian Community was not the monolithic structure we see emerging in the Early Middle Ages but a wild hothouse bursting with experimental growth.

A startling array of options competed to become the mainstream of Christian thought during the Patristic Period (i.e., the era of "Church Fathers" c.100-450 C.E.). Some options within the Christian family included: Neo-Platonism, Gnosticism, Arianism, docetism, Origen's Universalism, Apollinarianism, Ebionitism, Modalism, Pelagianism, and various forms of asceticism and mysticism. Although none of these became the eventual "orthodox" position, each contributed to the richness of Western Civilization and the Christian Faith. Any of these branches could have become the majority faith. The developmental process leading to medieval Christian dogma was evolutionary, with various species competing for a niche in Christendom.

However, the medieval Church insisted that it alone represented orthodoxy (Greek, *ortho+doxa*, literally *"straight opinion"*). Medieval Christianity's position was much like someone who had shot an arrow at a barn, then drawn a bull's-eye around the feathered shaft and declared it had flown true and straight to target. Any number of viewpoints could have carried the day. The battle-scarred consensus that became medieval Christian theology defended itself by continuously denying that other options were ever possible, because all views of the Faith that were contrary to the doctrines of the "Church Universal" were declared unfaithful to Jesus Christ. This, of course, is historically untrue.

3. Some Christians have always held these views.

If you have read this slim volume of Church history, you already know that quite a few early teachers and authors anticipated the principles of New Thought Christianity. While Baptists and Catholics can point to St. Augustine as their source for Original Sin and the total depravity of humanity, New Thought Christianity finds a hero in Augustine's foe, Pelagius, who held a more optimistic view about the perfectibility of men and women. Fundamentalists may preach hot hell for all non-believers—which, by the way, drew its images from Greco-Roman paganism, not Hebrew thought—but New Thought Christians find a more congenial figure in the thoroughly optimistic Church Father Origen of Alexandria. For example, Origen's Universalism was so complete that he insisted the mercy of God required even Satan to be saved! Trinitarians side with Athanasius in naming Jesus as the unique Son of God, but we find the arguments of Arius more compelling when he speaks of the Son as adopted by God, making him similar to God and yet very much like all of us.

Some Church Fathers speak of the vast gulf between a Holy God and sinful mankind, but Metaphysical Christians are *panentheistic monists* who believe in God as One Presence and One Power, like the fifth century Christian author known only to history as Pseudo-Dionysius the Areopagite. This unknown author, writing under a new pen name drawn from an obscure New Testament character, spoke about Divine Mind, the Silence, and the non-existence of evil—and Dionysius did this enlightened work at the leading edge of the Dark Ages.

Even a cursory review of historical theology shows that the central ideas of New Thought Christianity were not invented in the nineteenth century, although many of the religious organizations which teach Christian Metaphysics trace their origins to that time frame. The organizing date is merely a reflection of administrative significance and of no importance theologically. The United Methodist Church, United Church of Christ, Unitarian-Universalist Association and the Christian Church (Disciples) all have foundation dates in the twentieth century, but no one who understands history would seriously accuse the Methodists, Congregationalists, UU's or the "Disciples" of being Johnny-come-latelies. The same is true of the Association of Unity Churches International and Religious Science organizations.

4. We believe in and teach the Bible faithfully.

Too many New Thought ministers have problems convincing people—even their own members—that New Thought Christianity is solidly biblical, mostly because the fundamentalists have managed to define the terms for the general public. However, it has been my experience that the groups whooping the loudest in their wild admiration for the Bible generally understand it the least. Yet, the biblicists have been so effective in getting their misunderstandings before the public that narrow-minded, anti-modern views of the Bible have become the standard.

Pop Quiz: Which of the following *must* someone believe in order to be a faithful follower of Jesus Christ?

a.   Every word of Scripture was written by God.

b.   Complete internal agreement exists among biblical authors.

c.   All biblical stories and theology are internally consistent.

d.   The "good book" is historically accurate in all matters.

e.   Christian believers must accept the literal truth of every word of the Bible or they are being unfaithful to the biblical witness and rejecting God, Jesus, and the Church.

f.   None of the above.

The correct answer is *[f] None of the above,* because the first five points are scripturally, historically, theologically and rationally incorrect. The Bible, like any topic to be explored, should be approached without bias and with eyes open. Consequently, here are some of the assumptions from which modern biblical scholarship begins:

1. The Bible is the word of people, not the inerrant word of God; it records the fallible memories of people like us.

2. The Bible is not a book at all but an *anthology.*

3. Oral and written elements which came together as the Bible were composed and edited by a lengthy chain of people, almost all Jewish men.

4. These men wrote and edited their works, which later became scriptures, to reach specific target audiences who are long dead.

5. Authors wrote for specific religious, liturgical, political, and social reasons, some of which make little sense today.

6. Historical accuracy was seldom the goal.

7. The text provided a means to convey the authors' and editors' message.

8. Most importantly, the Bible *must be allowed to be what it is.* The only "authority" the Bible has is when God's Truth speaks through the imperfect words of our ancestors in the faith directly into the mind and heart of the individual reader today.

This is a vastly different set of assumptions than the average person holds about the Bible, and here we encounter the main difficulty in presenting New Thought Christianity as a biblical faith. Even those who utterly reject fundamentalist values often unconsciously accept the fundamentalist view of the Bible as the official Christian position, and therefore reject the Scriptures and Christianity, too. This happened because the Religious Right has been able to define what the Scripture is, how it must be approached, and what it means. *Says who?*

I was flying back from a conference when the man sitting next to me noticed I was reading Bishop John Shelby Spong's *Rescuing the Bible from Fundamentalism.* When he asked me a few simple questions, I replied warily, not wanting a cross-continental duel with someone who might assign me to the ranks of Satan's legions. My fears were unfounded; it quickly became apparent this man was quite open-minded. In fact, he had actually renounced Christianity years ago because he assumed there was only one way to look at the Faith of Jesus, i.e., the straight-and-narrow proclaimed by the Christian Right.

As we spoke, I became a littler bolder, and finally began talking freely about what historical scholarship has learned about the backgrounds of the Bible, the concept of looking for contextual meanings instead of insisting on inerrancy, and the obvious fact that different biblical authors held contradictory views. He was enthralled, and we spoke for hours. What really struck me about our conversation was that this intelligent, well-read, early-middle aged professional—who holds a master's degree in computer science, lives on Long Island and makes a six-figure income—*had never heard of any other way to look at the Christian faith, the Bible, and religion!* His total opinion of Christianity came from his Catholic parochial school upbringing and the conservative Protestant evangelists on TV and radio. Having no idea there were other options, so he had abandoned the Christian faith.

Frankly, who could blame him?

Progressive Christians everywhere should take this incident as a call to service, because there are literally *millions* of people in the Western hemisphere alone who would be delighted to know there are other options within that family of religions identified by the generic expression *Christianity*. Which brings us to the final point.

5. New Thought Christianity: Faith for the Future.

Anti-modern, narrow-minded versions of Christianity continue to offer people reduced contact with the real world, requiring them to slip into "Church-World" every Sunday, where the laws of science and reason no longer apply. This may have some appeal in times of widespread violence or political upheaval, but life in the future may present more attractive benefits than can be obtained by retreating to a pre-scientific worldview. For an endangered species like evangelical fundamentalism to exist requires an intellectual and social ecosystem that the modern world is progressively less likely to provide.

Fundamentalism is a dinosaur in search of a tar pit. In the twenty-first century, narrow-minded biblicisms will not likely provide the means, as demanded by the Book of Ephesians:

> ...to equip the saints for the work of ministry, for building up the body of Christ, until we all attain to the unity of the faith and of the knowledge of the Son of God, to mature manhood, to the measure of the stature of the fullness of Christ.[19]

I firmly believe in the power of the Christian message to transform lives, today and forever. New Thought Christianity may not be the only way to God, but it is a way that works for many people. Whether it's called *New Thought Christianity,* or *Metaphysical Christianity*, or just Christian mysticism—these ideas are not new. The mystical-metaphysical tradition represents a legitimate, historic branch of the Christian family tree with roots stretching back to the earliest days of the Faith. New Thought offers a spiritual approach that applies to everyday life, explains the nature of Reality, and offers hope for the future. It is biblically based, using the best techniques of modern scholarship and fearlessly allowing the Bible to be what it is—whether we agree with the biblical authors or not—rather than trying to re-interpret the Scripture for the purpose of proof-texting current church doctrines with biblical authority. New Thought Christianity gives us the power, as incarnations of Divine Mind, to read Scripture faithfully and yet affirm, occasionally: "Yes, that's what it says—*'slaves, obey your earthly masters with fear and trembling'*—but I don't agree. Things have changed."[20]

Most Metaphysical Christians believe in God as One Presence and One Power, just as some other Christians have believed throughout history, and New Thought people are not afraid to say *"some other Christians,"* having the courage to admit that there has never been anything approaching a unanimous view on the faith of Jesus, except a unanimous desire to serve God in Jesus' Name.

The next time someone calls New Thought by the derogatory term *cult*, a better response for Metaphysical Christians might be to hold their heads up high and say, "We follow Jesus Christ, teach from the Bible, and pray to the

---

19. Ephesians 4:12-13, *NRSV.*
20. Ibid, 6:5.

God in Whose image we are made. If that makes us a cult, at least we know we're in good company."

APPENDIX B

Study Guide

Introduction: A Short Course in Epistemology

1. What is "epistemology" and why does the author begin here?

2. On the second page of the Introduction the author says: "Any study of the Christian faith that does not face the ghosts in the basement will be unable to point to the angels on our balconies." Who are some of the "ghosts" in your religious basement? How about the "angels" on your balcony?

3. What characterizes religious "mystics" and why have they been such a challenge to church establishments?

4. Surprisingly, the author sounds almost sympathetic to "religious hierarchies" in their struggle to control the excesses of zealous believers. How can the tools of theology help both mystics and traditionalists clarify their questions and reach reasonable conclusions?

5. What "lesson" can we learn from Martin Luther's battle with church traditions?

6. List and describe the four formative factors in theology.

7. Someone says to you: "I just go by what the Bible teaches. I don't have any other 'factors' in my theology." How do you reply? Are these four reference points inescapably part of everyone's theology?

8. New Thought Churches pride themselves in being non-traditional. Is that completely true? Identify some of our traditions (e.g., doing guided meditations).

9. Which of the four formative factors in theology do you think is most important for Metaphysical Christianity? Explain.

10. Why does the author think his readers will be amazed when they learn about the beliefs and practices of the people he discusses in this book?

PROJECT: Before reading further, list every theologian, mystic and teacher you can name who taught Metaphysical Christian ideas and lived after the time of Jesus but before the twentieth century. (Keep your list for later.)

ALTERNATIVE: Write about your expectations for this course of study—what do you expect to learn?

Chapter 1—Philo Judaeus

1. Describe the first century C.E. city of Alexandria in Egypt.

2. Philo Judaeus tried to merge which two thought-worlds? What made this task so formidable?

3. How could Greek philosophy and the Jewish religion both be true if they were grounded in radically different ideas about God?

4. What did pagans and Jews have in common in regard to their religious legends and sacred writings?

5. Who was Zeno the Stoic? Give a brief account of his ideas. How did Stoicism help Philo? Do you find anything appealing in Stoicism today?

6. Explain allegorical interpretation.

7. What is the so-called *"Grand Allegory"* in Philo's writings?

8. Explain this passage: "...the events of scripture are intimate, personal happenings in the spiritual lives of everyone. They are parables of individual soul growth."

9. What was the purpose of Philo's mission to the Emperor Caligula? What was the result?

10. In what sense can Philo be called the "Father of Metaphysical Interpretation"?

CHAPTER PROJECT: Pick a brief reading—no more than ten verses—from the Torah, i.e., the first five books of the Old Testament. Do a metaphysical interpretation of the passage. (If you're bold enough, just throw open the Bible somewhere between Genesis-and-Deuteronomy and take whatever passage your finger lands on.)

ALTERNATIVE: Do a metaphysical interpretation of a Greek or Roman myth, fable, legend or well-known story (such as Homer's *Odyssey*).

Chapter 2—Origen of Alexandria

1. How did political and military events in the holy land affect the early Christian church? How did Rabbinic Judaism respond to this increasingly hostile world?

2. Some early Christian thinkers, like Tertullian of Carthage, denigrated classical studies and asked; *"What has Athens to do with Jerusalem?"* Do you agree? Explain and respond to this point of view.

3. Describe Origen of Alexandria. What kind of a man was he?

4. How was Origen *"the first true biblical scholar of our Christian heritage"*?

5. What kind of ascetic practices did Origen engage in which might be considered excessive today?

6. How did Origen's work correspond to the efforts of Philo Judaeus?

7. What is *"universalism"* and what did Origen say about it?

8. Explain the term *"Logos"*. What modern metaphysical expression is the rough equivalent of this Greek word?

9. What was Origen's method of interpreting Scripture?

CHAPTER PROJECT: To experience in a small way what the Christian ascetics did, take a vow of silence for one day. If you must speak, do so only when spoken to and conclude the conversation quickly. Keep a journal of your thoughts during the day.

ALTERNATIVE: Pick a prayer word and center on that word for a day. Every time your mind is not occupied with some task, go back to your word, repeating it again and again.

Chapter 3—Pelagius, Augustine and Hypatia

1. When the Roman society transformed from paganism to Christianity, how did the Christians treat pagans and heretical sects?

2. Explain the picture of Jesus seated on the rainbow as envisioned by the medieval church.

3. What two different views of life existed during the last days of the Roman era?

4. List three questions on which Pelagius and Augustine disagreed.

5. For each of the three questions you listed above, compare and contrast Augustine's positions with the views of Pelagius.

6. How did Demetrias, the daughter of a wealthy Roman, involuntarily cause the conflict between Pelagius and Augustine?

7. How prevalent was Pelagianism?

8. The author says that Augustine's point of view prevailed by "outright bribery." Explain what happened.

9. What great, world-shattering event happened in 411 C.E. that made Augustine's gloomy view of life seem more realistic than Pelagius's sunny optimism?

10. Who was Hypatia and what happened to her?

CHAPTER PROJECT: Write scene from a play in which Pelagius and Augustine debate their points of view. Or, write an original one-act play or short-story about Hypatia's life, including her martyrdom.

ALTERNATIVE: Find ten "Augustinian" passages in the Bible which seem to disparage human worthiness and respond to each with two passages supporting the Pelagian view that humans have free will and are basically capable of doing good. Which are easier to find?

Chapter 4—Pseudo-Dionysius the Areopagite

1. *"Large numbers of books, letters and treatises which assert themselves to be from the hand of a well-known figure are in fact from the pen of an unknown author writing much later under a pen name."* How might this basic principle of biblical interpretation topple the pillars of scriptural truth in the minds of some Christians? How does it affect your view of the Bible?

2. What examples of this principle can be found in the Hebrew and Christian Scriptures? List several pseudonymous works in today's Bible.

3. List some ancient Christian works which did not make the New Testament canon.

4. The work discussed in this chapter was pseudonymously penned. What New Testament character was the author portraying?

5. Give a few "New Thought" ideas which Pseudo-Dionysius sketched over fifteen hundred years ago.

6. What did Pseudo-Dionysius say about God as One Presence/One Power?

7. Describe the Dionysian theology of Evil.

8. Like modern Metaphysical Christianity, Pseudo-Dionysius held that God's essential nature is *impersonal.* How did this fifth century author describe God?

9. In chapter four, the author flatly states: "Any image of God, dreamed up by limited human intelligence, must necessarily be wrong." Do you agree? How, then, can anyone speak of God at all?

10. Discuss the similarities between Pseudo-Dionysius and other present-day metaphysical teachers. In your opinion, should we study him today?

CHAPTER PROJECT: Write a pseudonymous New Testament book of your own, taking the pen name of a biblical character. Follow your inspiration; it might lead you to compose a one-page epistle, or even a mini-Gospel.

ALTERNATIVE: Read an early Christian book that didn't make it into the New Testament. Prepare a proposal to include this in bibles of the future. Or, write a defense of the Church's decision not to include the book on the New Testament list.

Chapter 5—John Scotus Erigena

1. Why are Hebrew, Greek and Latin important languages for Bible scholars?

2. How did Latin go from being a language of the people to a private communication among church scholars?

3. What sort of man was John Scotus Erigena? Why is it significant that he was an Irishman?

4. Why did King Alfred believe nobody would be able to read the Bible in a generation or two?

5. What is *predestinarianism*, and why are its implications so important to Christian thought? Who were some of the greatest advocates of this position?

6. Who was Gottschalk, and why did Erigena get into trouble by debating him?

7. What connection brought John Scotus Erigena and Pseudo-Dionysius together? Describe Erigena's attitude toward the earlier author's work.

8. Trace the outlines of Erigena's picture of God. How big is his vision?

9. What is the *Big Bang Theory*, and how does it relate to John Scotus Erigena's doctrine of Divine Evolution/Involution?

10. Name the four stages in Erigena's grand scheme.

CHAPTER PROJECT: On a piece of blank paper, create a new Cosmos. Tell what principles you would set up to operate in your Universe. Remember, since you are re-creating time-and-space, *everything* is subject to change, even the basic laws of science.

ALTERNATIVE: Make an exhaustive list of arguments for and against *predestinarianism*.

Chapter 6—Meister Eckhart

1. Analyze and interpret this passage from the writings of Meister Eckhart:

   Nobody ever wanted anything as much as God wants to bring people to know him. God is always ready but we are not ready. God is near to us but we are far from him. God is within; we are without. God is at home; we are abroad.

2. How did Eckhart show a degree of tolerance to other religions which was uncommon in medieval thought?

3. As a bright child of poor parents, what was Johannes Eckhart's only route to an education and increased social status in the Middle Ages? What evidence do we have that he excelled in this profession?

4. What was *Scholasticism* of the Middle Ages? Explain how a knowledge of Plato and Aristotle provides a key to understand Scholasticism.

5. Who was Thomas Aquinas, and what was his major contribution to Christian thought?

6. It is said that Meister Eckhart applied the theology of Thomas Aquinas to his own life of faith. What were some of Eckhart's applications of Thomism?

7. How did politics of the Medieval Church play a role in Eckhart's troubles with orthodoxy?

8. Explain Eckhart's term *Seelenfuenklein.*

9. What three ways did he say we could know God?

10. When Meister Eckhart spoke of *becoming God*, what was he talking about? How does fallible humanity "become God"?

CHAPTER PROJECT: Write a poem about Meister Eckhart's life and work.

ALTERNATIVE: Find and listen to some music which could be Meister Eckhart's theme of life. Will it be classical, hymns, pop, rock, New Age, folk, Rap, R&B, Country, or something else?

Chapter 7—George Fox

1. Why was George Fox the "Cheerful Walker"? What was so dangerous about his times?

2. What changed Henry VIII from a Roman Catholic "Defender of the Faith" into a Protestant Reformer?

3. What was the "Middle Way" of Anglicanism? How are British Anglican churches supported to this day?

4. To whom did George Fox go, at first, when he was a young man struggling with his "exercises"? Describe the incident in Dr. Cradock's garden.

5. What happened on Pendle Hill? Summarize the Truth George Fox perceived. Is the Life Force in Nature the same as God?

6. How did Fox and the Quakers incur the wrath of their countrymen about hats? What kind of persecutions did they suffer?

7. What did Fox mean when he said all people had the "Inner Light"?

8. If Truth is one, how can radically different views of God be "inspired"?

9. According to George Fox, what kind of loyalty do Christians owe their governments? Why are most Quakers pacifists?

10. How did the contrast between the beliefs of Puritan New England and Quaker Pennsylvania outpicture in the demographics of those areas?

CHAPTER PROJECT: Go for a nature walk during which you look for the sense of Oneness and All-Encompassing Spirit which George Fox saw from Pendle Hill.

ALTERNATIVE: Hold your own "Quaker Meeting" by sitting in the Silence—alone or with others—for an extended period of time, at least 30 minutes. Write down your thoughts after the experience and share them with others.

Chapter 8—Hegel

1. Why does the author compare Hegelianism to a machine?

2. How important was Hegel to the development of New Thought Christianity?

3. What is the difference between *philosophy* and *theology*?

4. Explain Hegel's idea of *geist* or Spirit.

5. Define *monism*. What are the some problems with radical monism?

6. Contrast *Idealism* with *Materialism*.

7. What is *dualism*? How does Daniel Defoe's *Robinson Crusoe* illustrate the absurdity of a dualistic divine plan?

8. How does Hegel's thought provide a way to affirm the One/One Power without denying that suffering exists in the real world?

9. The author suggests seeing Hegel's system as First Force, Second Force and Third Force. Using this system, briefly describe the Hegelian Dialectic.

10. What other teachers discussed the triadic nature of reality before Hegel?

CHAPTER PROJECT: Find or make a symbol to illustrate *First*, *Second* and *Third Force* (e.g., the *Ying and Yang* symbol, which you can't use—think of another!)

ALTERNATIVE: Give an example of the Hegelian Dialectic at work in your life experiences.

Chapter 9—Emerson & Parker

1. Describe the confrontation between Lao-Tzu and Confucius in the sixth century B.C.E. Who were they; why was the meeting significant; and what was the gist of their disagreement?

2. Briefly summarize Ralph Waldo Emerson's background and professional experience.

3. What were some of the ideas Emerson advocated in his controversial "Divinity School Address" in the spring of 1838?

4. Marcus Bach nominated Emerson as the true father of New Thought. Do you agree or disagree with Bach's assessment of Emerson's importance? What evidence can you find in Emerson's words to support your viewpoint?

5. Analyze the following passage from Emerson's "Divinity School Address" at Harvard: *"But the word miracle, as pronounced by Christian churches, gives a false impression; it is Monster. It is not one with the blowing clover and the falling rain."*

6. What was Theodore Parker's connection to the Divinity School Address?

7. Why did Parker write his sermons with a gun on his desk?

8. How did Emerson's teaching about the divinity within every person affect Parker's attitude about slavery and women's rights-way back in the 1840's?

9. List and discuss some of the ideas Parker put forth in his sermon "The Transient and Permanent in Christianity."

10. How did Emerson and Parker build bridges? From where to where?

CHAPTER PROJECT: Read the full text of Ralph Waldo Emerson's *"Divinity School Address."* [Available at multiple online sites.]

ALTERNATIVE: Read Theodore Parker's *"The Transient and Permanent in Christianity."* [Also readily available online.]

Chapter 10—Eddy, Hopkins, & Brooks

1. What was distinctive about the way early Christianity treated females?

2. The author suggests that Christian Gnosticism presented contradictory views of women. Do you agree? Can you cite examples of both pro-feminist beliefs and gender bias in the writings and practices of the Gnostic Church.

3. What did the term "Christian Science" mean in the early days of the New Thought movement? Why did some groups abandon this phrase?

4. Explain the controversy surrounding Mrs. Eddy's "discovery" of the healing method she later taught as Christian Science.

5. Who introduced Metaphysical Christianity to Emma Curtis Hopkins? Name a few people Ms. Hopkins taught.

6. What belief did Mary Baker Eddy and Emma Curtis Hopkins share about the reality of matter? Critically analyze this point of doctrine, suggesting an alternative if you disagree.

7. The author interviewed several people who knew Nona Brooks personally. According to these witnesses, what was she like?

8. Discuss the central Truth which guided Nona Brooks.

9. Re-tell and interpret the story of Ms. Brooks and the snakes.

10. Nona Brooks said:

    "You'll never get well by thinking imperfection. Perfect God and
    perfect man, that is the basis. Not mortal mind and Immortal Mind!
    Not two but One, and that one, God. Perfect! Everywhere present!
    Not two minds, but *One, One, One.*"

Reply to this unequivocal declaration from your own theology and life experiences.

CHAPTER PROJECT: Start your own New Thought movement! Imagine
yourself as a metaphysical pioneer in the late nineteenth century. Give your
movement a name, a set of central principles, and a strategy for growth.
Where would you begin to send your teachers and church-starters at the turn
of the twentieth century?

ALTERNATIVE: Map out a strategy for expansion in the twenty-first century. What central principles would you espouse, and where would you plant
new groups?

Chapter 11—Paul Tillich

1. What was the "neo-orthodox" school of Protestant thought?

2. Discuss the major contributions of Karl Barth and Rudolf Bultmann to
    twentieth century Christian theology.

3. What did Tillich mean when he said God doesn't exist?

4. Define "ontology" and list some of the questions it tries to answer.

5. In what sense do Tillich and H. Emilie Cady agree about the nature of
    God? Explain their view.

6. How is God-talk always symbolic?

7. The author says good symbol "participates in the reality it is symbolizing." What does this mean?

8. Explain the Eastern parable about meeting and killing the Buddha on the road. Why would a devotee kill the Master-Teacher?

9. How have post-modern Christians re-interpreted the up-and-down language of the Bible into modern terms? What is problematic about thinking about a God Who is metaphysically "up there" or "out there"?

10. What might Tillich have said about Metaphysical Christianity's belief that God is One Presence/One Power?

CHAPTER PROJECT: Create or find some symbols that have religious significance to you. If they are pictures, arrange them on a poster board, or if they are physical objects, make a home shrine with your symbols displayed.

ALTERNATIVE: Go on line and find the web pages of several religious faiths (e.g., Baptist, Baha'i, Buddhist, Hindu, Jewish, Lutheran, Methodist, Muslim, Roman Catholic, Shinto, Wiccan, etc.). See what kind of symbols you can find at their web sites. (Remember: Symbols can be pictures, objects, or words.)

Chapter 12—Teilhard

1. Discuss the formal religious affiliation of Pierre Teilhard de Chardin? How warmly did his superiors receive his writings during his lifetime?

2. The author says, somewhat facetiously: "Pierre Teilhard's handicap was formal education." How can education be a handicap?

3. In what way did Teilhard try to integrate scientific and spiritual insights?

4. What comparison did Marcus Bach make between Charles Fillmore and Teilhard?

5. How do the walls of the Grand Canyon tell the story of life on Earth?

6. Evolution remains a controversial topic in some religious circles. Why do you suppose that is true, and how might Teilhard have responded to today's anti-evolutionist Christians?

7. Where does Teilhard say evolution is headed? Explain what he meant by the *"Omega Point"*.

8. According to Teilhard, what happens to human consciousness when we arrive at Oneness with the Divine?

9. Name some other "Friends" which the author says could have been included in this study?

10. In the "Afterword" the author suggests that the goal of life on this planet ought to be *"the upward quest for political, social and spiritual unity in the freedom what God has intended for all of us…"* Do you agree? Explain and defend your answer.

CHAPTER PROJECT: Although originally written for a Unity readership, this book has implications far beyond that limited audience. List some reasons this book might be studied in other churches.

ALTERNATIVE: Read something by or about Teilhard de Chardin. Make notes as you read.

APPENDIX C

Evolution of the God-Concept Viewed Theologically & Anthropologically

A Grossly Oversimplified but Handy Index[1]

Animatism—Some inanimate objects and natural phenomena are alive and conscious, i.e., the mountains have *spirit-force*, but not a distinct spirit or personality. [Latin = *animat(us)* breathing, animated, filled with life.] Mountains are "alive" like a forest is a living system.

animism—Belief that some objects and natural phenomena possess *souls*. Not yet fully developed into a deity, e.g., the mountain has a distinct consciousness, it is a spiritual being, but it is not yet a *mountain god* with history and myths.

---

1.   Note: There was no straight line of evolution from "lower" to "higher" concepts. All of the below can still be found in the 21st century. However, one may infer a general sequence. For example, ancient Israel apparently moved up the ladder from polytheism to henotheism ("No other gods before me...") to monotheism, ("Yahweh alone is God..."). Later Jewish mysticism approached monistic panentheism.

polytheism—Many gods with individual personalities, histories and myths, e.g., the gods of Mount Olympus.

henotheism—Belief in one supreme god among the many gods who demands to be worshipped either primarily or exclusively. Some scholars argue this describes early Israel, where the chief Hebrew deity orders the people to worship no other God "before" him, which is hierarchical but not necessarily exclusionary.

monotheism (a.k.a., *theism*)—Belief that only one Supreme Being exists; other spiritual entities (angels, demons, human souls, etc.) may exist but are not divine.

deism—Form of *monotheism* in which God created and ordered the Cosmos but does not intervene in the affairs of humanity.

pantheism—God is everything; the Divine and the Cosmos are a coextensive whole; its unitary form proclaims *God is the Universe*. Some variations of *pantheism* can accommodate multiple subordinate spirits, even evil powers, as long as the totality of Cosmos and divine are one and the same.

panentheism—Everything is *within* God, as a fish is in the ocean.

monistic panentheism—*Monistic panentheism* even goes beyond *pantheism* to include the transcendent and imminent; all the principles and laws of existence as well as physical matter, energy, and any spiritual realms which may exist. More than fish and ocean, God embraces the all the principles of chemistry and physics by which the ocean exists and operates. Applying the term to Fillmorean theology: *God is mind, idea, expression.*

About the Author

The Rev. Thomas Shepherd is an ordained minister with the Association of Unity Churches International who also holds ministerial credentials in the Unitarian-Universalist Association and the Congregational Christian Church. A Vietnam veteran, Shepherd was awarded the Air Medal, the Purple Heart, the Vietnamese Cross of Gallantry, and two Distinguished Flying Crosses for combat action as a medical evacuation helicopter pilot. He left the Army in 1972 to complete college and seminary studies, graduating *cum laude* with a BS in Education in Social Studies from the University of Idaho, and *magna cum laude* with a Master of Divinity from Lancaster Theological Seminary, Lancaster, Pennsylvania. Returning to active duty with the US Army in 1976, Chaplain (Captain) Shepherd ministered to soldiers and their families at military installations in Missouri, Alaska, Colorado, Germany and New Jersey before retiring from active duty in 1988. He has served as senior minister of Unity Churches in Georgia, South Carolina and California, and worked as Assistant Executive Director and Theologian-in-Residence for Johnnie Colemon's Universal Foundation for Better Living. In 2005 Rev. Shepherd assumed teaching duties in the Historical and Theological Studies department of the Ministry and Religious Studies program at Unity Institute, Unity Village, Missouri. He has written articles for professional journals and for *Unity* Magazine, including his popular Q&A column *"I've Always Wondered About..."* Shepherd writes science fiction novels under the pen name Thomas Henry Quell, also available from iUniverse Press.

Index

Absolute Good 36, 167

Adoptionists xviii

Alexandria 3, 4, 5, 7, 13, 14, 16, 17, 39, 40, 149, 157, 160, 161, 171, 178, 179

allegory xxv, 5, 6, 7, 10, 11, 12, 15, 24, 26, 65, 178

Anglicanism 86, 87, 184

Apostle 19, 47, 48, 52, 92

Apostle Paul 19, 48

apostles xviii, xix, 45, 46, 47, 48

Aquinas 21, 56, 72, 73, 74, 75, 183, 184

Aristotle 4, 19, 73, 74, 75, 123, 183

asceticism 22, 23, 170

association 109, 163, 164, 165, 172, 193

Athens 4, 5, 19, 49, 52, 73, 77, 179

Atom-Smashing Power of Mind 144, 158

Augustine 21, 29, 31, 32, 33, 34, 35, 36, 37, 38, 39, 41, 62, 64, 122, 167, 171, 180, 181

Bach 50, 144, 145, 150, 157, 186, 189

Barth 24, 132, 133, 134, 188

Bible xvii, xx, xxi, xxiii, xxiv, xxvi, 4, 5, 7, 8, 10, 12, 15, 24, 27, 35, 36, 39, 45, 47, 48, 55, 56, 58, 59, 64, 65, 86, 87, 91, 92, 93, 98, 132, 134, 138, 139, 149, 157, 158, 160, 163, 167, 172, 173, 174, 175, 178, 179, 181, 182, 189

biblical xi, xix, xxiii, xxv, 7, 8, 10, 11, 15, 16, 21, 26, 27, 45, 46, 48, 50, 52, 59, 65, 71, 73, 74, 76, 84, 132, 134, 135, 139, 140, 145, 157, 172, 173, 174, 175, 179, 181, 182

Bingham 126, 127, 128

Brooks ix, 97, 121, 123, 126, 127, 128, 129, 130, 149, 157, 187, 188

Bultmann 132, 133, 134, 139, 188

Cady 56, 97, 102, 108, 115, 126, 136, 157, 188

Caesar 7, 13, 14, 58, 121

Caligula 13, 14, 179

Catholic xix, xxi, 20, 36, 46, 59, 69, 84, 85, 86, 87, 130, 140, 142, 164, 165, 167, 168, 170, 174, 184, 189

Christ xiii, xvii, xviii, xx, xxii, xxv, 16, 18, 19, 23, 24, 25, 30, 34, 41, 49, 50, 62, 64, 67, 75, 83, 84, 89, 90, 93, 100, 106, 107, 108, 111, 113, 115, 122, 125, 132, 134, 137, 139, 142, 144, 146, 147, 148, 150, 154, 158, 164, 168, 169, 170, 171, 172, 175

Christ within 83, 93, 125, 137

Christian ix, xi, xii, xiii, xiv, xvi, xviii, xix, xx, xxi, xxiii, xxv, xxvi, 1, 8, 15, 16, 17, 18, 19, 20, 21, 23, 24, 25, 26, 27, 29, 30, 31, 32, 33, 34, 36, 37, 40, 41, 42, 47, 48, 49, 50, 51, 52, 55, 60, 62, 63, 66, 67, 68, 70, 74, 76, 77, 84, 92, 96, 97, 99, 100, 104, 105, 109, 111, 112, 113, 115, 116, 122, 123, 125, 126, 127, 129, 130, 131, 132, 134, 137, 138, 139, 140, 141, 144, 146, 149, 150, 153, 154, 159, 160, 163,

164, 165, 166, 169, 170, 171, 172, 173, 174, 175, 177, 178, 179, 180, 181, 182, 183, 186, 187, 188, 193

Christian Church xi, xii, xviii, 18, 19, 36, 62, 112, 126, 144, 172, 179, 186, 193

Christian Science 125, 126, 127, 163, 166, 187

Christianity xi, xii, xiii, xiv, xviii, xx, xxiv, xxv, xxvi, 4, 19, 21, 22, 23, 24, 25, 27, 28, 29, 30, 31, 32, 36, 37, 41, 42, 46, 49, 50, 51, 56, 60, 64, 65, 67, 70, 71, 72, 73, 78, 79, 80, 83, 96, 97, 103, 105, 106, 108, 109, 110, 111, 112, 113, 116, 117, 118, 121, 122, 123, 125, 126, 127, 129, 130, 131, 134, 138, 140, 141, 143, 144, 145, 146, 149, 150, 153, 154, 155, 159, 160, 163, 164, 165, 166, 167, 169, 171, 172, 173, 174, 175, 178, 180, 182, 185, 187

Christology 24, 48

Confucius 107, 108, 115, 118, 186

correlation 134

Cramer 126, 128

Crusoe 100, 101, 158, 185

cult 163, 164, 165, 166, 167, 168, 169, 175, 176

Cyril 40

demythologizing 132

devil xxv, 20, 25, 84, 100, 101, 165

Dionysius 42, 45, 48, 49, 50, 51, 52, 53, 54, 55, 56, 58, 63, 64, 78, 79, 99, 159, 171, 181, 182, 183

divine xiii, xv, xvi, xviii, xx, xxii, xxiv, xxv, 4, 5, 6, 9, 14, 17, 20, 24, 25, 27, 32, 33, 37, 39, 45, 49, 50, 54, 55, 57, 64, 66, 67, 69, 70, 73, 74, 75, 76, 77, 78, 90, 98, 99, 101, 102, 105, 106, 107, 109, 111, 112, 113, 115, 118, 121, 126, 127, 128, 130, 133, 134, 142, 148, 154, 157, 158, 167, 170, 171, 175, 183, 185, 190, 192

Divine Mind 5, 17, 24, 25, 49, 55, 66, 98, 99, 102, 105, 171, 175

Divine Order 5, 74

Divine Science xxv, 121, 126, 127, 128, 130, 157, 158

Divinity School Address 106, 110, 111, 116, 186, 187

docetism, 170

docetists xviii

dogma 117, 133, 170

Dominican 67, 69, 71, 72, 73, 79

Dyer 91

Eckhart ix, xxv, 30, 42, 56, 68, 69, 70, 71, 72, 73, 75, 76, 77, 78, 79, 80, 95, 130, 149, 157, 158, 183, 184

Eddy 97, 121, 123, 125, 126, 127, 158, 187

education xiv, 71, 143, 183, 189, 193

Ehrman xix, 48, 158

Elizabeth 85, 86, 126

Emerson xxiii, 66, 78, 80, 96, 105, 106, 108, 109, 110, 111, 112, 113, 114, 115, 116, 117, 118, 124, 127, 130, 140, 144, 145, 149, 150, 186, 187

emperor 13, 14, 19, 64, 121, 179

Enlightenment 80, 88, 89, 108, 131, 138

epistemology xiii, xxii, xxiii, xxiv, 177

Erigena xxv, 30, 42, 57, 58, 61, 62, 63, 64, 65, 66, 67, 78, 79, 95, 149, 182, 183

evil xvii, 5, 10, 25, 31, 33, 34, 39, 50, 51, 52, 53, 54, 56, 62, 63, 64, 91, 94, 99, 100, 101, 102, 103, 123, 130, 133, 164, 165, 171, 181, 192

experience xv, xvi, xxiii, xxiv, xxv, 4, 5, 12, 19, 27, 37, 72, 78, 89, 104, 111, 128, 133, 134, 137, 138, 142, 143, 172, 180, 185

Father 3, 4, 17, 21, 22, 24, 25, 32, 34, 42, 63, 76, 79, 86, 107, 109, 110, 130, 142, 145, 165, 171, 179, 186

Fillmore, Charles 158

Fillmore, Myrtle 97, 125, 126

first century xi, xiv, xxv, xxvi, 3, 5, 7, 10, 16, 17, 22, 48, 52, 59, 97, 121, 143, 149, 154, 163, 175, 178, 188

force xix, xxii, 13, 35, 38, 50, 53, 56, 63, 74, 95, 99, 102, 104, 105, 153, 184, 186, 191

Fosdick xxiii, 150

Fox, Emmett 150

Fox, George 66, 80, 83, 84, 86, 87, 88, 89, 90, 91, 92, 93, 95, 130, 149, 157, 159, 160, 184, 185

Fox, Matthew 158

free will 29, 32, 37, 41, 62, 67, 181

Freeman ix, 50, 78, 149, 154

fundamentalism 134, 173, 174, 175

fundamentalist xxv, 41, 153, 167, 173

geist 98, 185

Gnosticism 170, 187

Gnostics xviii, 122

God ix, xiii, xv, xvi, xvii, xviii, xxi, xxiii, xxiv, xxv, xxvi, 5, 6, 9, 10, 11, 12, 13, 17, 19, 20, 23, 24, 25, 26, 27, 28, 31, 32, 33, 34, 36, 37, 39, 41, 49, 50, 51, 52, 53, 54, 55, 56, 59, 62, 63, 64, 65, 66, 67, 69, 70, 72, 74, 75, 76, 77, 78, 79, 80, 83, 84, 85, 86, 90, 93, 94, 98, 99, 100, 101, 104, 105, 106, 108, 111, 112, 113, 115, 116, 117, 125, 126, 127, 129, 130, 131, 132, 133, 134, 135, 136, 137, 138, 139, 140, 141, 145, 147, 148, 150, 151, 154, 166, 167, 168, 169, 171, 172, 173, 175, 176, 178, 181, 182, 183, 184, 185, 188, 189, 190, 191, 192

Good News 28, 36, 56, 138, 170

Gospel 23, 32, 47, 66, 122, 168, 182

Gospel of Thomas 122

grace 32, 34, 38

Greek xxv, 3, 4, 5, 6, 7, 12, 19, 29, 35, 58, 59, 61, 64, 73, 77, 117, 147, 163, 164, 171, 178, 179, 180, 182

Ground of being 136

Gurdjieff 103, 105, 159

Harvard 109, 110, 111, 139, 186

headquarters xxiv, 93

healing ix, 56, 109, 121, 124, 125, 126, 128, 187

heaven xvi, xxii, 25, 31, 33, 75, 85, 101, 112, 123, 132, 139, 154, 168

Hebrew xxv, 4, 5, 7, 8, 21, 58, 59, 117, 171, 181, 182, 192

Hegel 80, 95, 96, 97, 98, 99, 101, 102, 104, 105, 111, 124, 130, 159, 185, 186

Hegelian 96, 97, 99, 102, 103, 104, 118, 186

hell xxii, xxv, 25, 26, 33, 36, 100, 101, 132, 171

Hellenistic xx, 7, 13, 16, 18, 23, 30, 38, 47, 121

Henry VIII 84, 88, 184

heresy xiii, xviii, xx, xxiv, 32, 35, 41, 63, 73, 79, 93

heretic 20, 35, 85, 86, 149, 169

holy xv, xvi, xvii, xviii, 4, 5, 7, 9, 11, 12, 23, 24, 35, 38, 52, 70, 98, 106, 117, 134, 139, 171, 179

Hopkins 121, 123, 126, 127, 128, 149, 159, 187

Hymn of the Universe 149, 150

Hypatia 29, 39, 40, 41, 180, 181

imago Dei xiii, 76, 168

Islamic 70, 131

Israel 4, 5, 8, 17, 18, 158, 192

Jerome 21, 34, 35, 39, 58, 59

Jerusalem 4, 12, 17, 18, 19, 179

Jesus xii, xiii, xv, xvi, xvii, xviii, xix, xx, xxi, 4, 14, 16, 18, 19, 21, 23, 24, 25, 30, 31, 34, 36, 40, 41, 46, 47, 48, 49, 56, 58, 62, 67, 73, 75, 89, 91, 107, 108, 111, 112,

113, 115, 116, 117, 122, 123, 124, 132, 134, 137, 139, 142, 149, 164, 167, 168, 169, 170, 171, 172, 174, 175, 178, 180

Jewish xvi, xx, 1, 4, 6, 7, 8, 14, 15, 16, 17, 18, 21, 47, 48, 70, 98, 173, 178, 189

Jews 4, 7, 12, 13, 14, 17, 93, 131, 168, 178

Johnson 30, 31, 32, 35, 38, 60, 159

Judaism 4, 5, 7, 13, 15, 16, 17, 18, 98, 179

Kantonen 147, 148, 160

kerygma 132, 134

Koine 58, 59, 64

Lao-Tzu 107, 108, 109, 115, 118, 186

Latin xvii, 30, 35, 39, 58, 59, 60, 61, 64, 69, 79, 109, 117, 144, 182, 191

Lectio Divina 11

Lessons in Truth 108, 136, 157

liberal 36, 37, 96, 109, 113, 131, 159, 165

Lord xv, 9, 18, 23, 55, 60, 69, 71, 79, 86, 88, 89, 90, 115, 122, 126, 136, 150

Luther xvi, xvii, xviii, xxi, xxiv, 21, 32, 61, 84, 85, 150, 177

Lutheran 86, 166, 189

Macquarrie 26, 102, 103, 150, 159

Marcionites xviii

Master xxiv, 53, 69, 73, 169, 174, 189, 193

McGiffert 24, 49, 64, 73, 74, 79, 159

medieval xiii, xxv, 17, 29, 30, 31, 34, 39, 41, 42, 43, 49, 52, 54, 59, 60, 62, 63, 64, 67, 70, 71, 72, 73, 74, 78, 80, 122, 149, 170, 171, 180, 183, 184

meditation xvii, xxiv, 11, 12, 49, 54, 78, 90, 107, 109, 137, 154, 165

metaphysical xiv, xxiv, xxv, xxvi, 3, 5, 7, 8, 9, 10, 12, 15, 24, 25, 28, 36, 37, 41, 50, 51, 52, 67, 70, 78, 80, 83, 95, 96, 97, 98, 99, 102, 103, 104, 105, 118, 123, 125, 126, 127, 128, 133, 134, 140, 146, 149,

150, 153, 158, 169, 171, 175, 178, 179, 180, 182, 187, 188, 189

metaphysics 11, 133, 144, 145, 172

Methodist xxiii, 157, 172, 189

Middle Ages xvii, 62, 67, 71, 72, 131, 170, 183

mind xxi, 5, 8, 9, 12, 14, 17, 21, 22, 24, 25, 28, 35, 49, 51, 55, 61, 64, 66, 75, 77, 78, 95, 96, 98, 99, 102, 105, 125, 129, 144, 146, 147, 158, 166, 167, 171, 173, 175, 180, 188, 192

miracle 112, 113, 186

miracles xvi, 37, 106, 111, 112, 113, 116

monism 99, 100, 101, 102, 185

monistic panentheism 77, 192

Monophysites xviii

Montanists xviii

Muslim 74, 98, 189

mystical xii, xiv, xv, xvii, xxv, xxvi, 10, 12, 15, 17, 23, 25, 26, 27, 41, 42, 49, 50, 52, 54, 55, 64, 68, 72, 79, 94, 123, 130, 134, 140, 143, 144, 145, 146, 153, 175

mysticism xiv, xv, xxvi, 12, 17, 42, 49, 50, 67, 70, 72, 95, 140, 150, 170, 175

mystics xi, xiv, xv, xxiii, 17, 25, 42, 43, 56, 69, 72, 76, 77, 80, 123, 149, 150, 153, 177

Nag Hammadi xx, 21

neo-orthodox 24, 131, 132, 188

Nestorians xviii

New Testament xvii, 11, 15, 17, 47, 48, 52, 56, 58, 77, 108, 132, 134, 159, 160, 171, 181, 182

Nicoll 103, 104, 105, 159

Niles xii, xxiv

nineteenth century xxiv, 74, 80, 96, 105, 108, 109, 111, 112, 114, 116, 118, 123, 131, 171, 188

noogenesis 147

Omega Point xx, 67, 146, 147, 148, 149, 150, 190

ontological 140

ontology 133, 135, 188

Origen xxv, 16, 17, 20, 21, 22, 23, 24, 25, 26, 27, 28, 39, 40, 41, 42, 78, 95, 132, 149, 158, 170, 171, 179, 180

orthodox xix, xx, xxv, xxvi, 11, 15, 20, 21, 24, 30, 31, 38, 58, 63, 67, 130, 131, 132, 149, 163, 164, 167, 170, 188

orthodoxy xviii, xxi, 21, 30, 31, 35, 64, 67, 79, 131, 132, 140, 153, 171, 184

Ouspensky 103, 105, 159

Paganism 20, 30, 46, 171, 180

pagans 30, 178, 180

paleontology 146

panentheism 77, 192

pantheism 77, 192

Parker 66, 80, 96, 105, 106, 108, 109, 114, 115, 116, 117, 118, 127, 140, 149, 160, 186, 187

Paul 17, 18, 19, 30, 32, 38, 45, 46, 47, 48, 49, 52, 53, 55, 60, 72, 73, 77, 90, 101, 122, 130, 131, 134, 135, 140, 147, 159, 160, 170, 188

Pelagianism 35, 38, 41, 170, 180

Pelagius xxv, 29, 32, 33, 34, 35, 37, 38, 41, 42, 62, 149, 171, 180, 181

Penn 86, 93, 159

Phenomenon of Man 143, 144, 145

Philo xi, xxv, 3, 4, 5, 6, 7, 8, 11, 12, 13, 14, 15, 16, 17, 24, 27, 39, 40, 42, 78, 95, 149, 157, 160, 161, 178, 179

Plato 4, 5, 7, 8, 12, 17, 47, 73, 75, 123, 149, 183

prayer xvii, 11, 12, 49, 50, 55, 67, 72, 78, 107, 109, 115, 116, 125, 129, 154, 180

predestination 29, 62, 63

prophet ii, xv, xvi, 16, 98, 115, 126, 141

Protestant xvi, xxi, xxiii, 36, 46, 62, 69, 84, 85, 86, 110, 130, 135, 140, 163, 174, 184, 188

Quadrilateral xxiii, xxiv

Quaker 92, 93, 185

Quell ii, 92, 93, 193

Quimby 124, 125, 126, 150, 158

reason ix, xxiii, xxiv, xxv, 10, 32, 37, 51, 63, 65, 67, 75, 101, 113, 126, 135, 174

Reformation xvi, xxiv, 80, 150, 160

reformer xxi, 62, 184

religion xiv, xv, xxiii, xxiv, 11, 30, 32, 64, 73, 75, 85, 88, 98, 101, 105, 107, 111, 116, 131, 133, 134, 142, 145, 150, 157, 160, 164, 174, 178

religious xi, xiv, xv, xvi, xix, xxi, xxii, xxiv, xxv, 3, 6, 10, 11, 12, 15, 18, 21, 22, 23, 25, 26, 30, 34, 45, 46, 61, 64, 70, 71, 72, 83, 84, 86, 89, 90, 92, 93, 94, 95, 96, 99, 100, 107, 108, 109, 115, 126, 130, 131, 133, 137, 138, 139, 142, 144, 147, 153, 159, 161, 163, 166, 167, 168, 172, 173, 177, 178, 189, 190, 193

Religious Science xxv, 126, 130, 163, 166, 172

resurrection 25

Romans 18, 51, 52, 122, 132

Rome xx, 3, 4, 13, 17, 18, 19, 27, 30, 34, 38, 39, 52, 58, 59, 60, 84, 85, 121, 160

sacrament 87

salvation xvii, xxi, 24, 28, 31, 33, 64, 108

saved 6, 25, 31, 59, 60, 74, 167, 168, 171

Scripture xvii, xviii, xxi, xxiii, xxiv, 5, 8, 9, 11, 12, 24, 26, 27, 36, 47, 52, 54, 58, 65, 116, 134, 172, 173, 175, 179, 180

Second Coming 25

Second Jewish War 17, 18

sin 22, 28, 31, 32, 33, 34, 37, 39, 125, 171

sinners 34, 166

sixteenth century xvii, xviii, xxi, 61, 84

Society of Friends 93

Socrates 40, 41, 47, 73, 123

soul xiv, 6, 8, 12, 13, 21, 24, 25, 26, 27, 31, 32, 34, 60, 69, 70, 72, 74, 75, 78, 88, 95, 111, 113, 117, 130, 179

Spirit xiii, xiv, xvii, 9, 15, 24, 26, 27, 30, 36, 50, 70, 76, 89, 90, 93, 95, 96, 98, 99, 102, 104, 105, 123, 127, 144, 148, 154, 185, 191

Spiritual xii, xiv, xvii, xxiii, xxv, 8, 9, 10, 11, 12, 21, 22, 26, 27, 30, 34, 41, 55, 67, 72, 75, 77, 78, 80, 87, 88, 90, 95, 97, 99, 108, 109, 116, 118, 123, 124, 125, 126, 128, 133, 135, 138, 139, 140, 142, 143, 153, 154, 165, 167, 175, 179, 189, 190, 191, 192

Stoicism 5, 8, 178

Stoics 5, 6, 24

Symbolic 10, 11, 15, 25, 50, 51, 55, 56, 62, 83, 137, 138, 188

symbolism xxv, 5, 9, 10, 12, 26, 50, 134, 137, 139, 145

Teilhard xi, xx, xxi, 66, 67, 130, 140, 141, 142, 143, 144, 145, 146, 147, 148, 149, 150, 166, 189, 190

terrorists 23, 121

theology ix, xiii, xiv, xvii, xx, xxi, xxii, xxiii, xxiv, xxv, xxvi, 20, 23, 24, 25, 26, 30, 32, 36, 38, 41, 47, 49, 51, 52, 55, 56, 59, 61, 64, 67, 71, 74, 75, 77, 78, 95, 96, 97, 98, 100, 118, 130, 131, 132, 133, 134, 137, 140, 142, 144, 149, 153, 160, 166, 167, 169, 171, 172, 177, 178, 181, 184, 185, 188, 192

Thomism 72, 184

Tillich 45, 48, 55, 72, 78, 130, 131, 133, 134, 135, 136, 137, 138, 139, 140, 147, 149, 160, 188, 189

tradition xxi, xxiii, xxiv, xxv, 7, 9, 21, 47, 49, 63, 64, 73, 74, 76, 87, 146, 163, 175

Transient and Permanent in Christianity 106, 116, 187

truth xi, xii, xv, xvi, xx, xxi, xxiii, xxiv, 4, 5, 8, 9, 15, 21, 23, 26, 27, 28, 32, 37, 49, 50, 59, 63, 65, 66, 70, 73, 74, 83, 89, 90, 92, 95, 98, 102, 103, 104, 106, 108, 112, 113, 115, 116, 117, 118, 122, 125, 127, 131, 132, 134, 136, 143, 151, 157, 158, 169, 172, 173, 181, 184, 185, 188

Tumpkin xxv

Twelve Powers of Man 95, 158

twentieth century xi, xxiii, 22, 24, 28, 55, 97, 108, 118, 130, 131, 132, 134, 135, 140, 143, 147, 159, 172, 178, 188

twenty-first century xiv, xxvi, 10, 22, 59, 97, 121, 143, 154, 163, 175, 188

Unitarian 36, 80, 108, 109, 110, 159, 165, 172, 193

Unitarianism 109

United Church of Christ xxii, 144, 172

United Methodist xxiii, 36, 164, 172

Unity ix, xii, xxv, 10, 64, 65, 79, 93, 96, 101, 102, 103, 109, 125, 130, 140, 144, 145, 151, 154, 157, 158, 163, 164, 166, 167, 168, 172, 175, 190, 193

Unity Institute ix, xii, xxv, 10, 193

Unity Magazine 193

Unity School of Christianity 166, 167

Universalism 16, 17, 20, 24, 25, 27, 36, 41, 70, 92, 93, 108, 109, 170, 171, 179

Universalist 109, 165, 172, 193

weltanschauung 96, 102, 153

Whitehead xv

worldview xxi, 19, 31, 73, 96, 97, 102, 174

Yahweh 17

YHWH 5

Zeno 5, 6, 178

978-0-595-32534-4
0-595-32534-3

Made in the USA
Middletown, DE
20 March 2019